A LIFE OF CRIME

A LIFE OF CRIME

The Memoirs
of a High Court Judge

Harry Ognall

WILLIAM
COLLINS

William Collins
An imprint of HarperCollins*Publishers*
1 London Bridge Street
London SE1 9GF

WilliamCollinsBooks.com

First published in Great Britain in 2017 by William Collins

1

A catalogue record for this book is available from the British Library

ISBN 978-0-00-826746-9 (hardback)

Typeset by Palimpsest Book Production Ltd, Falkirk, Stirlingshire

Printed and bound by CPI Group (UK) Ltd, Croydon CR0 4YY

This book is produced from independently certified FSC™ paper
to ensure responsible forest management.

For more information visit: www.harpercollins.co.uk/green

To Sally, for so many reasons.
'That's it, then'

'There are worse prisons than words'
Carlos Ruiz Zafón, *The Shadow of the Wind*

PROLOGUE

Chinese wisdom encourages us to take comfort that 'even a journey of a thousand miles begins with a single step'. But what if the journey is not one that lies ahead, but one of retrospect? Does that need less resolve – or more?

My life in the law was filled with so much that enjoyed a high profile at the time, and which has left a legacy of continuing interest, and sometimes fascination. That said, there is an obvious danger that, as a central actor in those dramas, my recall may now be corrupted by the erosion of the passing years. Or my account may be tainted by the temptations of egotism, or the lure of the apocryphal.

And so I have put off this moment for a very long time, until it has become very clear that I should either embark now, or never. I must do my best to tell it as it really was.

1

BEGINNINGS

What follows will be the odyssey of my life at the English criminal Bar and as a Queen's Bench judge, recounted through the prism of some of the more memorable trials in which I was involved. But every narrative must have a beginning, and my early years seem to me to be as logical a starting place as any. Wholly to ignore the first twenty-five years of my life seems to me, anyway, to leave a void. However accidental my ultimate choice of career may seem to have been, perhaps within my early years is to be found the seed bed out of which my future grew.

I was born in 1934 in Salford, Lancashire, of middle-class Jewish parents. They were never more than easy-going in their orthodoxy, and (save in my early days at school during the war) my religion never featured as a significant or oppressive aspect of my life. I was named (curiously) Harry Henry, after my paternal grandfather, who had died one month earlier. I know very little about him. He was by all accounts a kind, modest and hard-working man. He lived with his wife, Bessie, in Rutherglen, Glasgow, and was a councillor for the Gallowflat Ward in what was then the separate town of Rutherglen, serving for one year as its provost, or mayor. He made the improvement of educational facilities and standards his special interest. He ran a small business, selling smoking pipes and tobacco.

My father, Leo, was the oldest of my grandfather's three sons and a daughter. He was born in 1908 and left school at sixteen. Thereafter, he worked first in Glasgow and then in Manchester in a variety of generally mundane jobs until the outbreak of the Second World War. (For a short time he was a cub journalist for a national newspaper, and achieved temporary fame by riding pillion on the Wall of Death at a visiting circus.) He worked for some years for a very large mail-order company. That bred in him a deep-seated and lifelong aversion to working for anybody save himself. He was adamant that both my young brother, Michael, and I should become professional men. (Michael was to qualify as a doctor.)

At the outbreak of war in 1939, his extreme short sight meant he was excused military service. He spent the war years working as a supervisor at an ordnance factory near Leeds that produced military vehicles and ammunition.

Providentially, he found his true niche in life in his middle years. He had always been an avid reader of detective fiction. I can remember a monthly magazine devoted to the genre – *Black Mask*, which was always in our house. With the end of the war, and with no obvious employment in prospect, he decided to give writing a go. It was a courageous decision. He had a wife and three children to support, and no guarantee of success, but against the odds, it worked. His first offering to Collins publishers was accepted. Thereafter, until his death in 1979 he wrote under two pseudonyms some four detective novels a year. The royalties, while never very substantial, more than kept the wolf from the door. Above all, it fulfilled his fierce wish for independence.

My father's small stature may well account for the fact (which I only recognized after his death) that he never rid himself of deep feelings of inadequacy. Only when going through his effects did I gain true insight into his real self. Over the last ten years of his life he wrote and assembled a large collection of reflections on life entitled 'Thoughts while

Thinking'. To my distress, I realized from reading these that I had scarcely known my father at all. His musings are sometimes provocative, sometimes touching, often profoundly wise, and throughout suffused with melancholy. I read them with a growing sense of wonder, and with sadness. Among them, I found this – written a few years before he died:

> All my life I have been a failure. My one achievement is that I am now honest enough to admit it.

How often since I first read those words have I wished I could tell him how wrong he was.

My mother, Cecilia ('Cissie' to all her friends), was born in 1909 of Polish immigrant parents who at the turn of the century had fled the pogroms with their families, and later married in the UK. Like many other Jewish refugees, they settled in Leeds. (The city was then a centre for bespoke tailoring, and my grandfather Noah was a skilled tailor.) My maternal grandmother (another Bessie) never learned either to read or write in the English language. Noah could read sufficiently to master the race cards published in the newspapers. He was an avid gambler.

My mother was a physically attractive woman. She was denied any higher education, but was gifted with a considerable native intelligence, insight and a natural charm. Unlike my father, she enjoyed a wide circle of friends. From time to time she turned her hand to the writing of short stories, some of which were published in magazines such as *Argosy*. She was a regular and successful entrant to newspaper competitions for verse-writing.

It was in those prehistoric days that the free-standing spin dryer burst upon an astonished world. It was the size of a tiny waste bin, with a spout under which an empty bowl had to be positioned. You placed the wet laundry in the contraption in small quantities, and switched on, whereupon it would bounce about merrily on the kitchen floor while a trickle of water dripped out (sometimes) into the bowl. My mother won one such device with this (as I believe, profound) quatrain:

> Quick as a dream
> A spark, a stream
> Life – at life's end
> Must seem

On the day she died, she left the day's main *Daily Telegraph* crossword beside her bed, correctly completed. I have always believed that her literary talents exceeded those of my father, but the ethos of those days was such that she subordinated herself to him in the roles of wife and mother.

Those were my parents. I suppose that to most outward appearances they were a pretty ordinary provincial suburban couple, and in many ways they were. But they had undoubted talents and they shared an unshakeable mission to see their children receive every advantage that they had been denied. An obvious question in view of my future career as an advocate is to ask if either ever demonstrated an ability for public speaking. The answer is 'no'.

When Neville Chamberlain declared war in 1939 we were living in London. I can still remember hearing planes overhead, and being vaguely aware that they were German. Though I never asked my parents, I have often since wondered at their feelings as they listened to reports of Hitler's unstoppable progress to the French side of the Channel. They, along with all other Jews in this country, can have been in no doubt at all as to the fate that awaited us if the Third Reich conquered our island.

We were living in Wembley, North London when war with Germany was declared. I was just short of six years old. Along with a huge number of other youngsters living in cities deemed vulnerable to the Luftwaffe, I became an evacuee.

I was taken by my tearful parents to Euston station, tagged with a name badge, a gas mask in a cardboard box slung around my neck. I held a tiny suitcase, packed with such few pathetic items as amounted to a wardrobe for a six-year-old child. Thence I was dispatched to Kendal in the Lake District. I was looked after by a couple named Jackson for what turned out to be just a few weeks. They lived on a smallholding at Cartmel, a village near Grange-over-Sands, north of Morecambe Bay. I recall almost nothing of my time there. I do still however remember the contrast between that beautiful, peaceful, hill shrouded place and the North London suburban home I had left. I also remember with an involuntary shudder being made at breakfast to drink unpasteurized milk, warm and straight from the cow. I believed at that tender age that I would have preferred the hazard presented by the bombers.

It is not to disparage the kindness of so many people like the Jacksons when I say that, happily, my stay there was a short one. My parents and my very little brother left London and moved to Leeds, where my maternal grandparents had been living for many years, and there I joined them. My father began work (which continued until the end of the war) in his exempt occupation at the huge ordnance factory near the city. Leeds became my home until I left for university.

The remainder of my childhood and adolescence was passed in the city, mainly in a rented semi-detached house in suburban Roundhay, with a large park nearby. For ten years I attended Leeds Grammar School, one of the great northern centres of grammar school education. When I started there in 1942, the fees per term were seven guineas; when I left, they were fifteen guineas (approximately £250 and £400 in today's money). On one occasion, my mother pawned her engagement ring to pay my fees and those of my brother for that term.

It is strange for me now to recall that, although corporal punishment for young offenders (in the form of birching) disappeared from our criminal law halfway through my ten years at the school, we were no strangers to it in the institution we referred to as LGS. There were two masters who employed it. The swimming instructor kept a piece of chair leg, known to all of us as 'mutton chop', that was soundly applied to the wet bum of the last of the class to get out of the pool after the whistle had been blown. The other devotee of similar violence was a bachelor classics master whose motivation I long ago recognized sprang not from a wish to instil discipline, but was beyond doubt the product of perverted sexual instincts. His incessant use of a very long, cylindrical ink ruler on the backsides of his charges was well known and widely feared. He called this weapon 'Algy', and would presage its imminent use with the hissed words 'Algy's barking.' Mercifully, he was feared no more after he overstepped the mark with some unruly and very big fifth-formers. They seized him and dumped him bottom first into a very large and deep wicker wastepaper basket so that he was helplessly wedged with his arms and legs up in the air. He was thus found, out in the corridor, by no less a person than the headmaster. It shows how distant was the era when this regime held sway, that it was an accepted commonplace in nearly every boys' school in the land, and that no parent ever sought to demur.

I ought to say that this aspect of my schooling should not only be seen in the context of its time, but pales into insignificance when I acknowledge all that the school did for me. My teachers, especially in my last three years, were outstanding. My parents' sacrifices in sending me there still fill me with wonder. I owe both them and LGS an enormous debt of gratitude for the way in which they fitted me for later life.

The school had some 800 boys. I remember that it was well known that the governors restricted the annual intake of Jewish boys to 10 per cent of the total. My first years there – until the end of the war – were the only time that I felt the scourge of anti-Semitism. Adult Jews were seen as draft dodgers, and had a reputation for using their business acumen during times of acute shortages to profiteer on the 'black market'.

From the snide comments regularly aimed at me and others, it was easy to guess the sort of observations being made at home by their parents. Life is full of ironies. I was living in a country that at the time was totally committed to the destruction of everything represented by the Third Reich – and by no means least, Hitler's 'Final Solution of the Jewish Problem'.

The head of the school was Dr Terry Thomas, known as 'TT', although any resemblance to the well-known stage and radio comedian of the same name was entirely coincidental. He ruled (and I mean *ruled*) the school for thirty years, the last ten of which coincided with my time there. Like all of us at LGS, I was in awe and fear of him. How well I still can see in my mind's eye the scene at the end of each term when all 800 boys assembled in the grand, pseudo-Gothic hall upstairs called Upper School. At the end of proceedings 'Fritz' Turner, the music master, played the piano as we all lustily and with total incomprehension sang in Latin the

school song: 'Floreat per saecula, schola Leodenses . . .' As
the last notes died away TT would say 'Have a good holiday,
boys,' and from 800 uplifted faces, unanimous in their insincerity, would come the response 'Same to you, sir.'

But, despite his awesome presence, it is to an encounter
with the headmaster in my penultimate year at school that,
as much as anything, I owe my future calling as a barrister.

When I was seventeen my father took me to see him for
an assessment of my chances of getting into Oxbridge if I
stayed on at school for an additional year. Neither of us ever
forgot his reply.

'The reports I have,' he said, 'suggest that your son has
not learned a great deal, but that he has a talent amounting
almost to genius for making what little he knows seem a
good deal more.' As we walked to the tram stop to go home,
my father said to me that this pointed possibly to a career
at the Bar. And that is how it happened.

After that, I never gave thought to any other option,
including the profession of solicitor. For me, that side of
legal practice seemed too cerebral, too closeted an existence.
I had no connections at all with the Bar, nor did we know
of anybody who could help me along that road. It was simply
that I instinctively knew that was the way for me to go. Not
for the only time in my life, I was lucky.

I went up to Lincoln College, Oxford in the autumn of
1953 to read law. Looking back, I have always cherished the
privilege of being an 'Oxford man', but there has also been
another side to that coin for me. I rowed and played tennis
for my college. In my last year, I was President of the
University Law Society. I made good friends. Despite all
that, I still feel that I worked too hard, and did not make
as much as I should have done of the many freedoms offered
by undergraduate life. Weekends were often quite lonely.
College chums with money – and there were still plenty of

them in those days – would take themselves off to the flesh-pots of London, and the tolling of many church bells on Sundays did nothing to lift my spirits. Perhaps my memory plays tricks?

The exciting news came in my last summer term, when I was offered a year's scholarship to the University of Virginia Law School to write a comparative law thesis for a Master's degree. I was fortunate to receive a Fulbright award to fund my travel expenses.

I spent a very happy year in the USA, during which I travelled extensively. It gave me a lasting affection for so many things that great nation has to offer. My brother and sister and my younger son all live there. My wife and I are frequent visitors, and we hugely enjoy the time we spend in California with our grandsons.

In those days one could read for the final Bar examination by correspondence course, and (working from home) that is what I did. As every intending barrister must do, I joined one of the four Inns of Court (in my case, Gray's Inn), and regularly travelled the 200 miles to London to fulfil the requirement of dining in hall on a stipulated number of occasions. Having passed the final exam, on 25 November 1958, wearing a dinner suit rented for the occasion from Moss Bros, I bowed before the Treasurer of the Inn, who called me to the Bar.

The summer before I went into chambers for the first time, I was invited by Mr Justice Pearson (later a Lord of Appeal) to be his marshal on circuit in the Midlands. (I had met him when I was at Oxford.) A marshal is a kind of *aide de camp* to the judge, and occupies a purely ceremonial position. I stayed in the local judges' lodgings with him, and accompanied him in sitting on the bench, and so got my first glimpse of what my future was about. It was a fascinating few weeks. I never forgot his kindness.

I joined chambers in Leeds, and became a member of the North-Eastern Circuit, to which all those practising in Yorkshire, Durham and Northumberland belonged. It exercised a modest disciplinary function, but at its core it was a giant freemasonry for all of us who fought against each other forensically by day, and caroused together by night in regularly held Bar messes in cities up and down the Circuit. Those of us who travelled the Circuit also came to know every decent eating place on offer wherever we went. The barrister who practises in criminal courts has as his essential work of reference Archbold's *Criminal Pleading and Practice*. One of the boon companions of my later days at the Bar was Peter Taylor QC, later to become no less than Lord Chief Justice. It was he who advised me that there were two essential books to be carried on our professional travels – an out-of-date Archbold, and an up-to-date *Good Food Guide*!

I became a pupil in Vince's Chambers in Leeds. As protocol dictated, my father paid 100 guineas to Alter Hurwitz, head of the chambers, for me to undertake a year's pupillage with him. My status as a pupil did not prevent me from accepting instructions to draft pleadings or from being briefed as an advocate – provided anything was offered to me. I had no independent means, which meant it was imperative that I should begin receiving work from solicitors, either in private practice or otherwise, as soon and as frequently as I could. But I was unknown to them. How was this to be achieved? The answer lay in the hands of the clerk to the chambers. There you took pot luck.

In short, the clerk was the interface between the barristers in the chambers and those who wished to instruct them. In those days, they received 10 per cent of all fees earned by 'their' barristers. Unless the solicitor in question asked for a particular barrister, it was left to the clerk to decide who he would favour with a case. In trivial cases, such as driving without due care and attention, the solicitor would not usually be concerned with the identity of the youngster chosen to conduct the case. They left it to the clerk. So you can readily see that for someone like me the clerk's power of patronage was enormous. I was fortunate that in those very early days my clerk, Frank Davies, took a shine to me. I thus received a fair number of otherwise unassigned instructions.

Of course, once the door was thus opened, it was up to me to prove my mettle. Receiving further instructions from the same source, but this time with my name on them, was what mattered. And so, by this means and by word of mouth, a reputation may ever so slowly start to build.

2

AN OPENING DOOR

Sited directly opposite Leeds Town Hall, where at that
time the higher courts were located, Vince's Chambers were
Dickensian in character. The rooms were on an upper floor,
approached via a gloomy wooden staircase that bore the
ravages of time. It was there that I undertook my pupillage,
having a go at any instructions given to my pupil master, as
well as (I hoped) tackling any work that came to me. I stayed
there for just a few years before being persuaded to join a
much busier set in the city.

My first chambers were certainly not fashionable. By that
I mean that they had no real foothold in anything but the
criminal courts, small civil actions in the County Court,
and undefended divorces. Common law chambers in theory
offer services in a wide variety of areas: criminal law, negligence (mainly personal injuries), contract, family law and
(very occasionally) administrative law. Of these, personal
injury litigation was by a distance the source of the largest
number of cases other than crime. In the main at that time
were claims for industrial injury sustained by workers in
factories or in coal mines. The work flow came to the Bar
either via trade unions (who were the plaintiffs) or insurers
(the defendants). There was a good deal of snobbery
attached to this work. In my young days, unless chambers
were favoured with it, they were viewed as down-market.
Certainly, a barrister without a substantial civil practice
could not be optimistic about a successful career, still less

about advancement to the rank of Queen's Counsel or the bench.

Divorce as an area of practice was never for me. Matrimonial disputes often generated passions beyond all reason, and the lawyers were always cast in the role of scapegoats. I did not mind the trivia of undefended divorces before a County Court judge. They were relatively well paid, and wholly untaxing. And they had their humorous moments. I remember a petition for divorce which contained the allegation that 'We were married on the 1st March 1961, and we separated on March 4th 1961. During that time, we gradually drifted apart.'

But when it came to disputes over money, and especially the custody of children, I cried 'halt'. And 'cried' is a wholly appropriate word for the experience which proved the defining moment for me in my rooted aversion to acting any more for husbands or wives in that arena.

I represented a husband in what proved to be a highly acrimonious and emotional contest over the custody of his two infant children. He lost; his wife was granted custody, with only limited weekly access being permitted to my client. Some few days later, I opened the morning paper to read that he had availed himself of that access in the most terrible fashion. He drove himself and his children to a country lane near Leeds, connected the exhaust to the car interior and so murdered them, also killing himself. Even now, as I write these words, the anguish that came over me at the time remains with me. There are occasions when to speak of professional objectivity is to defy human experience.

It followed that the chambers where I started my professional life was on the face of it unlikely to propel me onwards and upwards. Fortunately (how often do I say that?), the criminal law to which its members were essentially confined fitted precisely with my temperament and aptitudes. I was destined for the criminal courts. As a new boy, that meant the magistrates' courts. Then, as now, the greater proportion of criminal cases are disposed of there. Motoring offences, minor assaults, and a wide variety of petty offences of dishonesty are their lot. For a young advocate, they are an invaluable apprenticeship.

Unlike the procedure in the higher courts, the defence generally has no idea of the detailed evidence to be presented by the prosecution until the case gets to court. Thinking on your feet is an imperative. And another difference is that if (as frequently happens) things don't go too well, the consequences for the client are rarely serious.

I recall my many appearances in those courts not for the generally trifling nature of the cases, but for so many occasions where humour took pride of place over dignity and formality. I remember the sheer fun. It came unexpectedly, but even now –more than half a century on – I remember some of them with unrestrained delight.

As it happens, the first had nothing to do with crime. Pocklington is a thriving market town in what was once the East Riding of Yorkshire, about forty miles from Leeds. It is often described as the gateway to the Yorkshire Wolds. It has a well-known public school – and a magistrates' court.

On a cold winter's day during my pupillage year I went there to represent a young man in Affiliation Proceedings. This process was used if an unmarried woman became pregnant and alleged that a certain man was the father. If she satisfied the magistrates as to her claim, then the man would be ordered to pay weekly maintenance for the child until it reached the age of sixteen. Of course, this was long before DNA made issues of this kind obsolete.

The tiny courtroom was heated only by a coal fire, regularly and noisily stoked up by the court usher when not occupied with other tasks such as swearing in a witness. The girl gave her account, my client having been her boyfriend. At the relevant time, they had been in her parents' house. The parents went to bed, leaving the young couple in the sitting room downstairs. The girl alleged that it was then that they had unprotected sexual intercourse.

I called my teenage client, an agricultural labourer of limited intellect. 'The girl says that on that night you had sex with her on the sitting room sofa after her mam and dad had gone to bed. Is that true?'

'Yes I did.'

'Did you take any precautions?'

'Yes, of course.'

'What precautions did you take?'

'I wedged a chair under the sitting room door knob.'

Humour (intended or otherwise) was not the monopoly of witnesses. One morning I was sitting in Dewsbury Magistrates' Court, waiting for my case to be called. The defendant in the dock was addressed by the chairman.

'Young man, we see that you are not legally represented.'

'No, I'm not.'

'The charge against you is quite a serious one. We think that you should have legal aid so that your interests can be looked after.'

'I don't want it. The Good Lord will take care of me.'

'The bench thinks that you would be well advised to have the services of someone who is better known locally.'

This prompts me to say that there were indeed advantages in being represented before the magistrates by an experienced local solicitor who appeared frequently before them, rather than by a member of the Bar, who might have been thought to have the edge as an advocate. I learned that lesson in my very early days. The experience still brings a rueful smile to my face.

I was instructed to represent a bookmaker in an application before magistrates at Leeds for a betting office licence. There were objections, but suffice it to say that on any impartial view of the merits, the application was bound to succeed. The objectors were represented in court by Jack Levi, a very well-known Leeds solicitor, whose extensive practice often involved his personal role in representing clients before local benches.

The appointed day came. The magistrates came into court. As protocol dictated, all those legally involved stood up until the bench was seated – in this instance, all except Jack Levi. At once, from a seated position, he addressed the chairman of the bench.

'Please excuse my rudeness in remaining seated, Your Worships,' he said. 'The fact is that I have been very poorly.' (Repeated thumping of his breast with a clenched fist.) 'My doctor has advised me that I should take a break. But when I discovered that my opponent was to be represented by a rising young star of the local Bar, I felt that I owed it to my clients to turn up and do my very best on their behalf. I hope that you will understand.'

The chairman responded. 'Of course, Mr Levi. We fully understand. We are concerned for you, and you may remain seated throughout the hearing of this application, whether dealing with witnesses, or addressing the court.'

Do I need to tell you the outcome of the application? I prefer not to do so, though the phrase 'defeat from the jaws of victory' may give you a clue.

I am unsure whether what took place is properly characterized as a demonstration of part of the art of the advocate, but (like so many other episodes during my times in those courts) it was something I never forgot!

In another court in the West Riding of Yorkshire I was before a bench renowned for its toughness. At the end of my submissions, I placed heavy reliance on the burden of proof 'beyond reasonable doubt'. I was heard out with scarcely concealed impatience. The members of the bench put their heads together for a very short time. It was clear to me already that the lofty principles of English criminal law had come up against a brick wall.

The chairman said to my client, 'Stand up. We have listened with great care to what your barrister has said to us. We have to say that in this case we *do* have a doubt – but we are most certainly not going to give you the benefit of it.'

Acting for an Alderman of the City of Leeds, stopped by the police when driving erratically home from a civic reception, a police sergeant gave the following evidence: 'We overtook the car, and switched on our "police-stop" light. I walked back to the car. The defendant – who I see and now identify in court – was in the driving seat, alone. I opened the driver's door. There was a powerful smell of alcohol. I said to him, "I am a sergeant of police, will you please get out of your car, sir?" The defendant smiled at me: "Why, sergeant, is there another party?"'

Acting for a youngster who had been stopped one night by a police officer in Birkenhead because his car was showing no tail lights, this was a PC's evidence: 'I asked the defendant to come with me to the back of his car. He did so. I pointed out that there were no illuminated lights. The defendant gave the boot of his car a hard kick, whereupon the lights came on. He then smiled at me, and said "There we are, officer, all's well that ends well, eh?"

'"Very good, sir," I replied. "Perhaps you will now give your windscreen a similar kick and it will then display a valid tax disc."'

On my side of the Pennines, vehicle rear lights also featured before Wetherby Magistrates' Court. The police had followed a truck for some two miles. It displayed no tail lights. They stopped the truck, took the driver – my client – to the back of it, and pointed out the offence. The defendant scratched his head and said, 'Lights be buggered. Where's my bloody trailer?'

A witness before the Bradford bench: 'I drove along the M602, heading for the centre of Bradford. I lost my way, and at the end of the motorway I saw a man walking his dog and asked him if he knew the Bradford turn-off. "Know it?" he replied. "I bloody do. I've been married to her for thirty years."'

An important factor in some instances is for the court to know whether the witness before them is giving his or her testimony freely or under compulsion. Hence this exchange in York Magistrates' Court between prosecuting solicitor and witness:

'Is your appearance here today due to a witness summons?'

'No, I'm very sorry. I was late this morning and I didn't have time to shave.'

I must acknowledge with sadness that the room for joyous experiences like those is almost certainly no longer to be found before a bench of lay magistrates. The ethos has changed. There is an increasing emphasis on professionalism in the training of those who sit. It is no longer enough for a legally qualified clerk to advise the bench on matters of law; the bench must now be inherently 'judicial' in doing the job. There are also complex legislative restraints on their powers, for example regarding juvenile offenders.

In my own experience, this has deterred many who might otherwise have sought appointment – and caused some who have sat for many years – to quit. Common sense, maturity and worldly experience were in my day the criteria for appointment and continued fitness for office. Nowadays, it seems to me that a Justice of the Peace is treated as though he or she had a legal education and background. But they are not so equipped, and I dare to suggest that it is their 'lay' status that gives them the qualities that should matter. Since the huge majority of offences in our country are disposed of before magistrates' courts, those who visit them (under compulsion or otherwise) should be encouraged to find a community between themselves and those who sit in judgement on the less serious offences that form the calendar. Ordinary folk should be dealt with at this level by other ordinary folk. It makes for a less resentful, and therefore less divisive and better-ordered society.

Well, those were happy days, and a vital part of the learning curve of any aspiring advocate. I look back on them with gratitude and huge affection. But they soon fell away as I began to gain a toehold at Quarter Sessions and even sometimes at Assizes, when visiting High Court Judges sat for periods of some weeks in all the major cities on my circuit. This period of my life contained two events that came as a great relief to me.

The first was that the Homicide Act of 1957 marked the beginning of the end for capital punishment in this country. By 1965, hanging as a form of punishment was abandoned, and in 1969 it was abolished. The burden of defending someone who faced the death penalty if convicted fell only upon Queen's Counsel, and I was and still am eternally grateful that I never had to bear that dreadful responsibility. I remember talking to some who had the traumatic experience of going down to the cells after the judge had put on the black cap, and saying a literal goodbye to their client.

I ought also to acknowledge that for a judge presiding

over a murder trial, the duty imposed on him to pass sentence following a conviction must for many – if not all – have proved an equally fearful burden. The defendant, surrounded (and often physically supported) in the dock by prison officers, was confronted by the judge, who wore a black silk square placed on his wig. The High Sheriff and his chaplain (both robed) were alongside. The judge was then enjoined to address the defendant in these archaic terms, which were only slightly modified in 1947:

> [Name], you have been convicted of the crime of murder. You will be taken hence to a lawful prison, and thence to a place of execution and there be hanged by the neck until you are dead. Thereafter, your body be buried within the precincts of the prison. May the Lord have mercy upon your soul.

The chaplain endorsed this incantation with an 'Amen'.

It is difficult for me to imagine the pressure that participation in this macabre ritual must have imposed on all those involved. In at least one instance of which I am aware a very distinguished QC (Gerald Gardiner – later Lord Chancellor under a Labour administration) declined appointment to the High Court for fear that he would be called upon to pass the death sentence.

I must say something more about capital punishment, not least because in these most troubled times, where acts of terrorism are our constant companions, it would be remarkable if there were not a groundswell of public opinion in favour of restoring the death penalty. I do not share that view. My approach is founded both upon pragmatic considerations, born of a lifetime in the law, and upon a strongly held personal conviction. As to the former, I offer the following.

First, there is the well-rehearsed risk of a miscarriage of justice – and one that is beyond repair. However rare such cases may be, I find it impossible to reconcile myself even to one such instance.

By way of notable example, many will still recall the case of Regina v Craig and Bentley, tried before Lord Goddard, Chief Justice, at the Central Criminal Court in 1952. It may be an extreme example, but I remind myself of the aphorism that 'hard cases make bad law'. Christopher Craig was sixteen years old; Derek Bentley was a mentally retarded nineteen-year-old, an epileptic with a reading age of four who had been adjudged unfit for military service due to mental retardation. Both burgled a warehouse. Craig had a loaded pistol. (Significantly, Bentley was carrying a knife supplied to him by Craig, but never produced it at any stage.) The pair were confronted by a number of policemen on the rooftop of the building, one of whom urged Craig to hand over his weapon. The evidence that was obviously accepted by the jury was that at about this juncture Bentley shouted to his accomplice, 'Let him have it, Chris.' Craig fired the pistol, and killed one of the police officers, PC Miles.

Both youths were charged with and convicted of murder, on the basis of joint enterprise. The law, however, was that nobody under eighteen could be hanged for a capital crime. So it was that Craig was sentenced to life imprisonment (and was released after serving ten years). Despite the jury's plea for leniency, the Home Secretary declined to intervene. Nineteen-year-old Bentley (who did not fire the shot) was hanged. What did 'Let him have it, Chris' mean? Did it mean 'shoot', or did it mean 'Do as the bobby says, and hand over the gun'? On this nuance of language, Bentley went to the scaffold.

After a campaign led by Bentley's sister for nigh on half a century, in 1995 Bentley was granted a royal pardon, expunging the death sentence – but not overturning the conviction. In 1998, an appeal court did just that. The Chief Justice, stating that the trial judge, Lord Goddard, had failed to direct the jury adequately on the issue of joint enterprise, in respect of whether Bentley's cry just before Craig fired the fatal shot meant that, whatever his original intentions, Bentley wanted no further part in the criminal enterprise.

Bentley's sister had died one year earlier. What comfort was it to her in the last year of her life to know that her brother should never have been hanged, or to die not knowing that at last he was to be exonerated of murder?

In that immediate context, it is especially interesting to note that, in R v Jogee in 2016, the doctrine of joint enterprise in homicide was the subject of a substantial reappraisal by the Supreme Court. The court held that the doctrine had been wrongly interpreted and applied inappropriately in directions to juries for over thirty years. How fortunate it is that no one had been hanged on the basis of joint enterprise as wrongly understood by the lower courts during that period because, of course, capital punishment had already been abolished.

I also remind myself that for some years after 1957 the death penalty (although substantially abolished) was still in force for those, for example, who killed 'in the course or furtherance of theft'. You may have thought that the words 'course or furtherance' were plain English, and brooked of no ambiguity. If you did think that way, you would be wrong. It led to repeated argument in the Court of Criminal Appeal, on which the issue of whether or not the guilty party should hang depended on the study of etymology as much as upon the evidence. The confusion that successive decisions created was a powerful factor in leading ultimately to the total abolition of capital punishment. What did I say about the nuances of language?

As to the deterrence argument, my experience suggests that very few murders are the product of true premeditation. The killer rarely considers the consequences before the fatal act. And – going back to where I started – the terrorist actively *seeks* martyrdom.

Finally, and irrespective of all the above, I reject the principle of 'an eye for an eye'. It is a matter for each one of us to examine our consciences and ask whether we find state-authorized killing a justifiable exception to the injunction that 'Thou shalt not kill'. You know where I stand on that.

———

The second source of relief was a purely personal one for someone like me, who in those days, if defending, generally did so under the auspices of legal aid. In the early 1960s, the level of legal aid fees was greatly increased. With a wife and burgeoning family now to support, that was very good news for me.

The 1960s passed for me with a rapidly growing and increasingly demanding workload, mostly standing on my own feet, but on many occasions being led by a QC. To listen to the best advocates conducting a case to which I was privy gave me a wealth of experience, and growing confidence.

Two cases of my life as a junior are perhaps worth recall. Their status in my recollection is in part due to their circumstances, but also because I was led in the first by Gilbert Gray QC ('GG'), and in the second by Peter Taylor QC. They were the two colossi whose advocacy – in utterly different ways – provided my exemplars in my first years as a jury advocate. As I note elsewhere, Peter Taylor ultimately became Lord Chief Justice. That is surely quite enough to serve as a testimonial to his prodigious talents. GG receives his own special mention much later in this memoir, and he is the subject of my first account.

KEITH KITCHING AND GEOFFREY ELLERKER

Bully boys in blue

The defendants were both officers in the Leeds City police – our client, Kitching, a uniformed sergeant; Ellerker a uniformed inspector. Both were stationed at Millgarth Street police station in central Leeds. (Quite separately, Ellerker was to serve a prison sentence for assisting in a cover-up involving a police superintendent who had committed the offence of causing death by dangerous driving.) They were tried before Mr Justice Hinchcliffe and a jury at Leeds, I think in 1970.

The prosecution was led by John Cobb QC. He was an exceptionally able and hard-working Silk, later to be appointed to the High Court, but sadly to die shortly afterwards. Tall, thin and of ascetic demeanour, his written opinions frequently contained the phrase, 'I have given this matter long and anxious consideration.' It is perhaps not surprising that in those circumstances he soon became known among his colleagues as 'long and anxious Cobb'.

I digress. David Oluwale was a Nigerian vagrant who in the late 1960s was well known in Leeds city centre. He slept where he lay, in shop doorways or other such areas as might afford him shelter. He was classed as a dullard, and in 1965 he had been hospitalized for a time after a diagnosis of schizophrenia. He had been before the courts on several occasions for the sort of offences you might expect – drunkenness and breach of the peace. To most citizens he was a nuisance, but one which was tolerated. But not to our client or his co-accused inspector. The evidence showed that they detested him, and took a sadistic pleasure in harassing and humiliating him. If Kitching found him sleeping rough, he would summon Ellerker and the pair would assault him. On two occasions, they took him in a police van and dumped him on the far outskirts of the city. In the last twelve months of his wretched existence Oluwale was arrested five times. In each instance Kitching or Ellerker (or both) were involved in some way. Shortly put, they had it in for him.

On 18 April 1969, shortly after 5 a.m., two uniformed policemen were seen by an early-duty bus conductor in The Calls, a part of Leeds that in those days was semi-derelict. His attention was drawn by the fact that they were apparently chasing another man in the direction of a road called Warehouse Hill. At one end that road was a cul-de-sac, bounded by the River Aire. I am not consciously playing with words when I say that the road was a dead end; it was for David Oluwale.

The compelling inference is that it was he who was fleeing from the two policemen, and that in so doing he fell into the river and was drowned. Three weeks later, his body was recovered from the river some miles downstream. Its condition by then precluded any assessment by the pathologist of whether, when still alive, he had been assaulted in any way.

At the subsequent trial, with characteristic and scrupulous thoroughness John Cobb's team established that all the police officers on duty in Leeds on that night could say exactly where they were at the time spoken of by the bus conductor – that is to say, all except Kitching and Ellerker.

The Director of Public Prosecutions (DPP) decided, on counsel's advice, that both men should not only be charged with other offences of assault on Oluwale (and with a related offence, in one instance, of perjury), but that there was sufficient evidence to charge both with manslaughter of the unfortunate man. The basis for that charge lay in the argument that it was they who had chased Oluwale into a place from which they knew he had no escape, and that they recognized that his death in the river was the likely outcome.

It is unnecessary for me to set out the legal or evidential reasoning that led to what followed. Suffice it to say that the judge directed the acquittal of both men on the charge of manslaughter, as well as of perjury. In the end, however, they were both convicted of two offences of assaulting Oluwale in order to occasion him actual bodily harm. Kitching was sentenced to twenty-seven months' imprisonment; Ellerker to three years.

The case came at a time when public confidence in the city's police was at a low ebb, and subsequent events showed that the prosecution was a timely and effective deterrent to any further misconduct of this nature. It was also, no doubt, a very early signal to our society that racially engendered prejudice would be rooted out and punished.

On a personal note, it was an education to me to see both Cobb and Gilbert Gray in action for some days, along with a close understanding of the issues. Cobb – angular, meticulous, studied, ruminative and grave; Gray – avuncular, instinctive, colourful and ever the pre-eminent thespian. I learned much from both, and was ever grateful.

———

In November 1972, again at Leeds, I was led by Peter Taylor QC in what was to be my last major trial as a junior. I took Silk the following April. Since it was my last case of note in which somebody else's guiding hand was on the tiller, I suppose that even if it had not been intriguing with respect to its own facts (which it was), it would still deserve inclusion here.

JOHN MICHAEL AND SHIRLEY ELIZABETH REED
The elusive motive

One of the fundamental principles of English criminal law is to be found in the classic definition of the concept of intent. Juries are invariably directed to bear in mind the clear distinction between, on the one hand, motive, and, on the other hand, intent. The example I used to adopt in this situation when I was sitting was to say to the jury, 'Suppose that you saw a man point a loaded gun at his victim's head at close range and pull the trigger. You may have no idea at all of his motive, but you will have no difficulty at all in deciding his intent.' The terms of that direction have an uncanny application to the facts in R v Reed (JR) and Reed (SE).

Before I summarize the facts, I want to say this. Obviously, serial murders are in a wholly different category of depravity by virtue of their repetition – if for no other reason. But that said, in the times of which I write, this case is as chilling a story of a brutal death as can be imagined.

John Reed had a long criminal record, with a string of convictions for dishonesty. They included two for robbery with violence. For the latter of those, in 1966, he had been sentenced to seven years' imprisonment, from which he was released on licence after four years. His wife, Shirley, had no convictions.

At the time of the murder their home was in Oldham, but (importantly) they had for some few months in the past lived in Halifax. The evidence suggested that they were in the habit of using taxis to get around.

Milton Walker was a Halifax man. He worked as a taxi driver from a rank in Bull Green in the town. On 29 March 1972 he was working a night shift. Having been seen in his

Ford Cortina taxi on the rank at about 11 p.m., he was never knowingly seen alive again. The evidence was to disclose that the 'Taxi' sign on the roof of the car had been removed before the vehicle was finally recovered.

Around 1 a.m. the following morning a car that was almost certainly the taxi in question was seen by a witness close to the place where subsequent discoveries were made. A man and a woman were inside it. There was no taxi sign on the roof.

Within minutes, an explosion was heard. At 2.15 a.m. a man and a woman were seen on foot in the open country-side nearby. Shortly afterwards, the couple turned up, still on foot, at an isolated farmhouse (Doldrums Farm) on the moorland near Halifax. John Reed asked to use the phone, and summoned a taxi to take the pair to Oldham.

The next morning, the burnt-out remains of the Cortina were discovered. That same morning, a walker found the body of Milton Walker in (or close to) a disused quarry at Denshaw, high on Saddleworth Moor, some five miles from Oldham. His wrists and ankles had been bound with washing-line cord. He had been fatally shot through his forehead. Close by lay a spent .410 cartridge.

From the back of the Cortina was recovered a fairly old .410-calibre shotgun of Canadian manufacture. Its barrel had been shortened. Investigations established that the weapon had been bought by John Reed for a trifling sum a week before the murder from a pub acquaintance named Hickling, whose account of the deal was strenuously disputed at the trial but was obviously accepted by the jury. (John Reed had at first denied to the police any knowledge of the shotgun, and later pointed the finger at Hickling.)

At the Reeds' home was found a hacksaw that had been purchased a short time before by Mrs Reed. Swarf recovered from it by a forensic scientist matched the metal on the barrel of the recovered shotgun. In witness statements to the police made by each of them in May 1972, they firmly denied any involvement in the death of Milton Walker.

So there, in sum, we had the locality, the chronology, the sightings of a man and a woman, their appearance at Doldrums Farm, and the weapon and the hacksaw. Taken together, they presented a formidable case against the two accused.

At the trial, evidence was also given by a fellow remand prisoner who was facing a charge of unlawful possession of a firearm. He said that John Reed had told him that he too was charged with an offence involving a gun, and that he had admitted that in his case he had pulled the trigger.

After the prosecution evidence had been heard, it was submitted on behalf of Shirley Reed that she had no case to answer, or (alternatively) that the evidence implicating her was so tenuous as to make it dangerous to leave the case to the jury. The judge rejected that submission. Both were convicted. Both applied for leave to appeal. In October 1973 John Reed withdrew his application. I believe that he then made a statement to the police acknowledging his guilt, but seeking to exculpate his wife.

I say 'I believe' because although that is my information, I never saw the statement. Tellingly, after the Appeal Court granted Shirley Reed leave to appeal and heard her full appeal, no such statement was referred to by her counsel before the court. Giving the judgement, Lord Justice Megaw said that the court was satisfied that on the totality of the evidence more than one person must have been involved in the murder. Concluding that the trial judge was correct to reject the submission that he should stop the case against Shirley Reed, they dismissed the appeal.

So much for a précis of the facts. Now I must return to the beginning of this account. There can be no doubt at all that if it was proved that John Reed shot Milton Walker through the head and was abetted in that action by his wife, then both intended to kill him. It was akin to an execution. Both were thus undoubtedly guilty of his murder. But what was the motive for that dreadful act? Although motive is irrelevant in proof of guilt, this case is one of the very few – if not perhaps the only one in my own experience – where motive remains highly elusive. That there was a motive cannot be in doubt, and it must have been a powerful one. This conundrum is in itself sufficient to merit the inclusion of the case in my collection.

The police theory was that on that date the two were set upon committing a serious crime in Halifax, or thereabouts, and that for the purpose, they equipped themselves with the cord and the shotgun. At some stage, they wanted to leave Halifax. They went to the taxi rank and got into Milton Walker's Cortina. Then something went seriously wrong. The police believed that Walker, in the course of casual conversation, must have told the Reeds that he recognized them. Their nefarious purpose demanded their anonymity. That set in train his trussing, kidnapping and killing.

I have many doubts about this, not least because I remain unaware of any recorded serious crime committed in or near Halifax at the relevant time. It is true that there was some evidence that on the night concerned Reed may have had in his possession a suitcase or package, but this takes us no further. Moreover, I find it difficult to accept that, even if the Reeds were leaving the scene of a crime, they would choose to do so by taxi.

So, there it is. Something we may never determine, but something of real gravity and moment, prompted a fatal reaction in Milton Walker's last taxi fares on that night. It is impossible, isn't it, to imagine the sheer terror suffered by that poor man as he was driven, a bound and helpless prisoner in his own car, up to that bleak moorland. Did he know what fate shortly awaited him? That is why I say that this was a case of wickedness unlike almost any other in my encounters with evil.

With that, I shall leave the junior Bar behind me, and move on.

———

The Courts Act of 1971 abolished the old structure of Quarter Sessions, Assizes and Recorders, and replaced it with Crown Courts. Most Queen's Bench judges and Circuit judges sit in those courts to try crime. But a large part of the work is undertaken by Recorders – part-time judges in practice at the Bar, and a few solicitors with the relevant experience. I applied to become a Recorder under the new system, and was appointed in 1972.

The office of Recorder is of some antiquity. Until 1971 it was the perquisite of any city to appoint a practising member of the Bar of sufficient seniority to be its Recorder. In that office, he sat for some few weeks a year in the Quarter Sessions, dealing with crimes above magistrates' level, but excluding High Court work. In the counties, there were similar Quarter Sessions, presided over by a Chairman or Deputy Chairman. The Recorder (or Chairman) could invite any barrister called seven years or more ago to sit as one of his assistants. My first sitting was at the invitation of the Recorder of Middlesbrough, and I did the job a few times both there and elsewhere.

After the passing of the Courts Act of 1971, appointment to the office was at the instance of the Lord Chancellor's Department (now the Ministry of Justice). When, in 1972, Assizes and Quarter Sessions were replaced by Crown Courts, many suitably experienced barristers – juniors or Silks – were appointed Recorders on a nationwide basis (I suppose they would have numbered around 300). Their jurisdiction was much the same as that I have just described. Hence I found myself faced with trying alleged crime up to a very serious level (for example, causing serious bodily harm with intent, an offence carrying a maximum sentence of fourteen years' imprisonment). It was part-time, although there was an obligation to sit for at least four weeks per year. Generally, we sat on the circuit of which we were a member. In my case, however, for my first sitting in 1972 I was dispatched to Liverpool, where I sat in a building in Nelson Street, an adjunct to the main court premises in the grand St George's Hall. It was a memorable time for me, and not solely because it was my first sitting as a Recorder.

Two years later, Edward Heath, as Prime Minister, was to call a general election in a desperate effort to put an end to the industrial strife that was paralysing the country's industry. He was rash enough to take as his rallying cry the question 'Who governs Britain?' Well before then, the mine-workers, led by Arthur Scargill, had given him a resounding answer. They pulled the plug. For two weeks of winter in that dingy courtroom in Liverpool, we sat by candlelight. Heath lost the next election.

Most of that, my first sitting as an officially appointed judge, was occupied with a trial in which the defendant was represented by Rose Heilbron QC. An able, attractive and charming lady from Liverpool, she would become only the second of her sex to be appointed to the High Court. I came to know her and her delightful husband very well, when later each of us became Masters of the Bench at Gray's Inn. I was very relieved to learn that after her client's conviction she did not seek to challenge either my summing up or the sentence I had passed. Not that it should have mattered to me, or to any judge in the same position, but still, as a new boy . . .

One other case in those days served as a timely warning about the dangers of what the Bar knows well as 'Judgeitis'. It is when someone finds the bench an increasingly suitable vehicle for pomposity, or worse. In this instance, I was to sit with two lay magistrates (as sometimes happened). The case involved an appeal against the refusal by a chief officer of police of an application to renew a firearms certificate. The issue raised was purely a matter of law. In those circumstances, the matter was solely for me to decide, as the legally qualified member of the troika. The magistrates could play no part. After the arguments were concluded, we adjourned so that I could consider my ruling. I carefully prepared a written one. As no more than a courtesy to the two magistrates, I showed it to them before we went back into court. It transpired that one of them was a school headmaster. 'Well, sir,' he said to me, 'of course I can say nothing about the legal correctness of your ruling, but your grammar is very poor.' Enough said.

At Easter 1973, while I was on holiday abroad, my clerk phoned me to say that my next application had also been successful. I had been appointed Queen's Counsel. So it was that after thirteen years, my time as a junior barrister came to an end. That time had seen me involved in many adventures, but save for the two I have already described, none bear detailed repetition. I have decided that to include any more would be to put ego before any real curiosity value. I shall say to them thanks for the memories, and move on.

It is from the remaining chapters of my life in the law that this story derives its true substance. I was involved in many criminal trials of note. Their circumstances are at its core. From an extensive catalogue, I have chosen a number each of which I believe has a particularly compelling tale to tell. None will receive preface. They speak for themselves.

3

THE SILK ROAD

THOMAS ANDERSON

An ill-considered remark

In December 1974, at Leeds Crown Court, Thomas Anderson was tried for the murder of Daisy Elizabeth Morris. I led for the prosecution.

Daisy Morris was eighty-three years old when she met her death in April 1974. Her later years had been increasingly sad and solitary. She was a spinster who lived as a virtual recluse in a bungalow called Veleta Cottage, at Scarcroft, near Leeds. Her home for the last twenty-five years of her life, by 1974 it was little more than a dilapidated shack. (Her tiny income included a sum by way of annual royalties. In 1906 her great-uncle had composed the music and steps for a dance very popular in Edwardian times; it was called The Veleta.) The property included a small paddock. As a whole, it had potential for planning permission. Therein, it was submitted, lay the catalyst for the killing.

Anderson was by occupation a rat-catcher. He had ambitions to be an entrepreneur; in that, he was a failure. During 1973 he negotiated openly via lawyers with Daisy Morris and her brother for the purchase of the property. This came to nothing – not least because he offered a derisory price. Then he made a serious mistake. It was one that led to fatal consequences.

He borrowed £1,000 (£7,000 in today's values) from a business partner, on the false pretext that he had agreed the purchase of the property. He said that he needed the money partially to fund a deposit on the deal. In fact, he used the money to buy a car. When the partner found out, he successfully sued Anderson for the return of the loan, and obtained a court judgement for it in early March 1974. During March and early April, the sheriff took steps to enforce the judgement by seizing Anderson's available assets – including the car. He was persuaded to hold off for a short time, but the car was to be seized on 19 April.

In the course of these few weeks, the evidence showed, Anderson made several visits to the cottage. At his trial, he maintained that those visits were prompted simply by friendship and compassion for a lonely and wretched old woman. The reality (as the jury must have concluded) was that their true purpose lay in his increasingly desperate efforts to persuade Daisy Morris to sell her property to him – and at his offered price. Her continued refusal to sell must have led Anderson to snap. He saw this as the root of all his troubles. Frustration and revenge propelled him on. When Daisy Morris once more said 'no', she signed her own death warrant. She was last seen alive on 11 April 1974. Three days later, the visiting milkman found her body lying on the floor inside Veleta Cottage.

I said that Anderson made a serious mistake when he borrowed money that he could not pay back. In retrospect that was true. But it was not nearly as serious as the error that he was to make immediately following the milkman's discovery. This mistake alone singles out the case of R v Anderson as deserving inclusion in my catalogue.

It is noted in the field of criminology that perpetrators frequently cannot resist the temptation to return to the scene of their crime while it is still 'fresh'. If they do, they offer a hostage to fortune. While the milkman was still there, Anderson turned up at the cottage.

Here, I need to interrupt this story to set what followed in context. In 1974 Denis Hoban was a detective chief super-intendent in the Leeds police. Then fifty-two years of age (he was sadly to die only four years later), he was, in my profes-sional lifetime, one of the very best coppers I ever encountered. In the north, he rightly enjoyed a huge public reputation as a 'thief catcher'. His rank put him in effective charge of investigations into all major crime in the Leeds area. That included murder, and geographically it included Wetherby Road at Scarcroft, where Daisy Morris lived and died.

When, shortly after the milkman's discovery, Anderson turned up, it is very important to note that – for reasons that will soon become apparent – he did not go inside the cottage. He stood in the outside doorway. From that vantage point he could see the body. His first remark was to say to the milkman, 'This is a case for Denis Hoban.'

The evidence was to disclose that the deceased had been strangled to death by means of a ligature made of binder twine, knotted tightly around her neck and biting deep into the tissues. I say 'was to disclose' advisedly. The presence and nature of the ligature was only discernible on very close exam-ination of the body. Crucially, there was strong and reliable evidence that from where Anderson stood (with the milkman) in the outer doorway it was simply impossible to see anything that could afford any clue as to the cause of death. (This was such an important aspect of the case that the trial judge, Mr Justice Caulfield, supervised a visit to the cottage by the jury and all others involved in the case to inspect the layout.)

The sparse existence (for it could scarcely be described as a life) led by Daisy Morris – who, let us remember, was eighty-three years of age – dictated that she was under-nourished, and likely to be in fragile health. It was central to the case against the accused that in any normal circumstances, for her to be found suddenly dead would come as no surprise at all. Surely, the instant reaction of any ordinary observer would be that she had simply died a natural death. But these were not normal circumstances, and this was no ordinary observer.

The case for the prosecution was that in making his remark about Denis Hoban, Anderson disclosed that he knew that Daisy Morris had met a violent death. At that moment, and standing where he was, how could he have known that this was a case of murder – unless he was the killer?

Of course, that was not the only incriminating evidence. There was, in my opinion, abundant evidence as to motive, and the chronology was damning. No doubt, too, the jury did not take kindly to the accused's account of why he had made so many calls on Daisy Morris in March and April, very shortly before she died. (He was one of the most dapper dressers I ever encountered among the criminal fraternity. What was such an immaculately turned out man doing, consorting with that pitiful, unkempt old lady?) My cross-examination of Anderson was not a difficult task; I had plenty of ammunition. But I believe that his return to the scene and his remark to the milkman was all that was needed to make the case against him a conclusive one. The jury agreed.

And so, Thomas Anderson, aged seventy, became at that time the oldest person to be convicted in England of the crime of murder.

MICHAEL TAYLOR

Exorcism and two unanswered questions

I represented Michael Taylor at Leeds Crown Court in March 1975. Until the events in question, he was an unremarkable man, living in Ossett, West Yorkshire. Married, with no children, he was devoted to his wife. Then he fell in with a Christian fellowship.

Taylor was a vulnerable personality, and events led those within the fellowship to believe that he had within him what they described as 'demons'. On the night of 5–6 October 1974 at St James's church in Barnsley an Anglican priest and a Methodist clergyman subjected him to an all-night session after persuading him that he had the 'demons of murder' in him, which must be exorcized. At 6 a.m. they sent him home, but warned him that the demons were still within him. They had literally driven him mad.

At home, in that demented state, and in the belief that his wife was possessed of the devil, he attacked her with his bare hands with the utmost sustained brutality, inflicting upon her fatal injuries the nature of which were so appalling that they will here receive no further description.

At 10 a.m. that morning he was found in the street where he lived, stark naked and heavily bloodstained. He shouted that it was the blood of Satan. He pleaded not guilty by reason of insanity, and that was the verdict of the jury. The court made a hospital order.

Addressing the trial judge before the inevitable court order, I asked him rhetorically how those so-called ministers of God could now live with themselves, fastened with the knowledge of their responsibility. That was my first question. The second question is one that I have asked myself many times since those long-ago events. Michael Taylor was released into society after four years' detention: how could he live with himself once recognition dawned on him as to what he had done to the woman he had so dearly loved?

Many years later, I learned that he had subsequently tried on four occasions to take his own life. If I am asked again now to answer either of those two questions, I cannot really do so. But I have no doubt who would be the subject of my wish for absolution.

KALINDA CHAPMAN

Femme fatale

In 1978, at Newcastle, I led for the defence.

In a volume of John Betjeman's collected poems that I have cherished since boyhood there is to be found one entitled 'In a Bath Teashop'. It includes the pithy description, 'She, such a very ordinary little woman'. Those words exactly describe my first and abiding recollection of Kalinda Chapman. Yet the evidence revealed with chilling clarity that she was not only a calculating murderer, but a woman who held men in such thrall that they would do anything to engage and keep her favours – including doing her bidding to kill. And that is what two of her many lovers did. Her fatal powers over John Wright and Alan Stoddard led directly to the death of her husband, Brian, and to life imprisonment for all three who were complicit in his murder.

Kalinda was married three times. She bore four children. Brian was her third husband. She married him in 1976, and unsurprisingly they soon fell out. One stark factor in their discord was that she took in John Wright as a 'lodger'. In truth, he was her lover. They had first met when Wright was only fourteen, and living in a care home where she was then employed. He was infatuated with her. They had regular sex together. It came as no surprise that shortly after John Wright moved in, Brian Chapman left.

Kalinda saw divorce (to which she was no stranger) in the offing. She and Brian shared ownership of the house. She was determined that he would have no share of its proceeds. In that seemingly trivial motive were to be found the seeds of murder.

In Wright's subsequent confession he was to say that they talked about pushing Brian from the cliff top at Saltburn. That plan was abandoned. But before a second plan was devised, Alan Stoddard came on the scene as an additional paramour. Older than Wright, who was still only twenty-one, he was described as of limited intellect. He shared with Wright his infatuation with Mrs Chapman. At her continued instance, a second plan to kill Brian Chapman was set in train.

On the night of 29 April 1977, Kalinda lured her husband to a beach at Redcar. Pursuant to her plan, Wright and Stoddard lay in wait. They accosted Brian Chapman. The poor man must have known what fate awaited him. According to what Wright later told the police, Brian Chapman's last words were 'I knew this was coming. You'd better get on with it.' They did.

Kalinda held the two assailants' coats and watched as they attacked and killed her husband. He was strangled by Wright. His body was dragged into the sea. It was a feigned suicide.

The plan nearly succeeded. A pathologist concluded that it was a case of death by drowning. (He would later seek to explain his undoubted error by saying that the means of asphyxiation adopted by Wright would not necessarily leave any of the classic signs of strangulation.) Kalinda said that her husband was a depressive who had previously attempted suicide.

It was very soon after this that she brought down the whole house of cards upon herself. She took in another lover, and threw Wright out. His response was to say to her, 'You've just made the biggest mistake of your life, chucking me out.' He did nothing at that time to act on this threat, but the implication was obvious, and Kalinda was not without guile.

Aware of Wright's emotionally volatile state, she was determined to pre-empt any attempt by him to implicate her.

In July 1977, she volunteered to the police that she and
her husband had been walking innocently along the beach
when Wright and Stoddard confronted them. She witnessed
their homicidal attack on Brian. She had not reported it (she
said) because they had threatened her into silence. She denied
any part in the killing.

Wright and Stoddard were charged with murder. At that
stage, Kalinda could not be charged along with them. The
only evidence against her came from the two men, and in
law if they were all to be tried together, the evidence of her
co-accused would be inadmissible against her. Different
considerations applied, however, once the two men had been
convicted – as they were on 20 December 1977. If they
chose then to give evidence against her as prosecution
witnesses at a separate trial, that would in law be capable of
proving her guilt. That is what happened.

In January 1978, following their convictions for the
murder, both men made detailed witness statements impli
cating Kalinda as the authoress of the plot to kill. Wright
said, 'She wanted Brian dead, and me and Alan were stupid
enough to do it for her'; Stoddard that 'She wanted him
killing, and was there when he died. I was stupid enough
to carry out the murder on her behalf.'

Kalinda was arrested and charged with murder. In reply
to the charge, she said, 'It took you long enough. I've been
half expecting it. But I'm not worried. God will tell me what
to say.'

At her trial, Wright and Stoddard gave their evidence in
accordance with their statements. This confronted me with
a very difficult challenge. The best that I could do was to
rely before the jury on the indisputable principle that, since
both men were convicted murderers, the jury should be very

slow to convict on their evidence, unless they could find other material affording support for it – what lawyers call corroboration.

Here, too, Kalinda's own account to the police left very big questions unanswered. How came it that two men she knew intimately should do this? Was it simply a coincidence that they happened to be on the same beach at the same time as she and her husband took their walk? Why did she not report it to the police immediately?

I had a very experienced Newcastle-based junior, Rodney Percy. Both he and I were in no doubt that if our client went into the witness box and was cross-examined, the destructive impact on her case would be even more serious for her than leaving these already loaded questions in the air. We told her that the choice must be hers alone, but having heard what we had to say, she accepted the advice. She did not give evidence. (God was plainly not going to tell her what to say.) Her constant sobbing into a handkerchief as she sat in the dock left the jury unmoved. Kalinda Chapman was convicted of murder on what the trial judge described as clear evidence and sentenced to imprisonment for life.

This case makes its appearance in my gallery of trials because it shows that sometimes truth can be stranger than fiction – and equally compelling. It also serves as a graphic counterpoint to the outcome of my next case, where my client's exercise of his right to silence had a much happier outcome.

DOUGLAS MURRAY McCOMB

A blind eye?

In the early autumn of 1976 Douglas McComb was a deputy assistant governor at HM Prison Hull. At the time, the prison housed over 300 inmates, of whom nearly 50 were 'lifers' and the remainder were long-sentence prisoners. They were therefore men in whom protracted incarceration had bred increasing volatility of emotions, and a feeling that they had nothing to lose.

The catalyst for a violent eruption out of this simmering discontent was to be found in a number of factors. They included (in that prison) an increased use of Rule 43 solitary confinement by way of disciplining disruptive individuals, and a significant restriction in the permitted exercise facilities. For whatever cause, from 31 August to 3 September 1976 the prisoners engaged in a massive riot, and virtually destroyed 70 per cent of the prison. In those three days, they congregated on the rooftops, hurling slates and other materials down on the prison officers below. There was a suggestion that they had also thrown hand-made Molotov cocktails. It was at that time the largest and most destructive episode in British prison history.

Within the three days, the prisoners began a negotiated surrender. By the morning of 4 September all but seventy five of them had been transferred to other prisons. It was at that stage that Mr McComb came on duty. Of Class 2 governor grade, i.e. of no real seniority, he had only been assigned to Hull prison some three weeks earlier, and he had not been present at all during the riots.

On that morning, a group of prison officers determined to exact rough justice on the remaining rump of rebellious inmates by way of revenge. Their misconduct was later likened by a senior inspector of prisons to that of a 'mob trying to control a mob'.

When my client was interviewed by the police it was suggested to him that his total inaction during the behaviour of some of the 'screws' was a form of cowardice. In July 1978, the Director of Public Prosecutions advised that twelve prison officers, and Mr McComb, an assistant governor, be charged with conspiracy to beat prisoners.

At the preliminary hearing the stipendiary magistrate, Ian Boyd, accepted a submission that there was no evidence to support the allegation against my client – no evidence that he had agreed that violence should be used, or was party to it. The charge of conspiracy was accordingly dismissed. The magistrate rejected a further submission that the charge of neglect of duty should also be dismissed, though he did observe that on the evidence he had heard, others of supervisory grade could well have found themselves facing a similar charge.

Before the trial began, my instructing solicitors said that they had been able (on my advice) to find a witness with long experience in the prison service whom we might call as an expert on the issue in point. I met him at a hotel in York. He was a crusty former colonial civil servant, who had been the superintendent governor of the notorious Changi Jail in Singapore. Over tea and cake in the shadow of York Minster I invited him to say how he would have responded in my client's situation. With scarcely a pause, he said that the prisoners could consider themselves fortunate; they should have been shot. I thanked him very much for coming, but told him that I did not think we needed to trouble him further.

The defendants appeared at York Crown Court in 1979 in a trial that lasted some three months. The prosecution team was led by Peter Taylor QC. I was instructed to lead for the defence of Mr McComb, against whom the case was that he had deliberately turned a blind eye to the violence perpetrated by his subordinates, well aware what was going on. It was specifically alleged that he had deliberately failed to take any steps to prevent, stop or report the violence used by his subordinates. Thus it was alleged that by this deliberate omission to do his undoubted duty, he had wilfully condoned their conduct.

My task did not prove a particularly difficult one, as it turned out. We could show that Mr McComb had not been briefed on the turbulent situation in the prison when he came on duty. His lowly governor grade and relative inexperience meant that he was wholly out of his depth.

This, moreover, was a trial where I was in no doubt at all that my client should not give evidence. I was very confident that the story revealed my client (as the stipendiary magistrate had hinted) to be a scapegoat for the shortcomings of his elders and betters. My view was that he would be no better off if he gave evidence, and when subjected to the formidable talents of Peter Taylor QC under cross-examination, his situation might become a good deal worse. He accepted my advice.

In my closing speech, I submitted to the jury that the notion that he had either the experience or the perceived authority to prevent or stop this terrifying, vengeful mass misconduct was simply laughable. As to the failure to report what had been happening, would that not have been a devastating confession of his own unfortunate inadequacies? Eight prison officers were convicted by the jury; four were acquitted – and so was my client.

The case was remarkable in my experience for two reasons. First, I never either before or after that case encountered a body of prosecution witnesses whose bad characters offered such a fertile breeding ground to defending counsel seeking to demonstrate dishonesty or palpable bias as the motivation for their evidence. It reflects great credit on the jury that despite this, they were able to sort the wheat from the chaff and reach a series of rational decisions, convicting some and exonerating others. I shall speak elsewhere of my unshakeable faith in the jury system, but for now I offer this case as a prime justification of that faith.

Speaking of witnesses of bad character, by a most curious quirk of fate one of the prisoners called to give evidence for the prosecution was John Michael Reed, the life-sentence prisoner who, along with his wife, Peter Taylor QC and I (as his junior) had successfully prosecuted for murder seven years earlier. Thus it was that – uniquely in my experience – in 1979 Taylor called as a witness of truth a man who, in 1972, he had prosecuted for murder and whose truthfulness when he denied that crime he had emphatically and successfully challenged.

The second reason that I remember this case is that when my client had been acquitted and discharged from custody by the judge, he left the building in a flash. I never saw him go, nor did I ever hear from him afterwards. I was certain that in the event of conviction he would have been gaining a different perspective on life 'inside' from the one that his job had afforded him until that day. In those circumstances, was a 'thank you' in order?

In fairness to Mr McComb, it was in my opinion essential to portray him in court as an inexperienced and perhaps inadequate man, and maybe one who justified the police's suggestion to him that he had been a coward who was simply not up to doing the job. For him to listen to this must have been painful. The fact that it helped to secure his acquittal was perhaps, for him, not enough to make good the public humiliation?

I comfort myself with the fact that since the defence costs were funded under legal aid, at least my fees were paid.

PETER WILLIAM SUTCLIFFE

Mad – or bad?

The following account will receive a good deal of my attention. For that I make no apology, since it concerns what for me became the centrepiece of my time at the Bar. The unique status of the case in the litany of criminal trials in this country during the twentieth century alone justifies its pre-eminence here. It was to prove the most notorious trial in which I was to be cast in a leading role. So, both the public and the personal significance of the trial assuredly merit the profile that I give to it.

Such was – and remains – the impact of the case that it has over the past thirty-five years attracted an enormous body of media attention. Books have been devoted to it; countless commentaries and TV exposure have captured wide public interest. I am very conscious of this as I set to. Sadly, I am the last survivor of those who were intimately involved in its events. To my knowledge, none of the others who shared the stage with me published their thoughts, and so I believe that for that reason my contribution will not be seen as plagiarism, but rather as lending a worthwhile additional dimension to an understanding of the drama.

On the evening of 2 January 1981, Sergeant Robert Ring of the South Yorkshire Police, accompanied by a probationer constable, was on routine motor patrol on the outskirts of Sheffield. They were close to a large house used as business premises during working hours. The officers noticed a Rover car parked in the driveway. Sergeant Ring decided to check it out. There were two occupants. In the front passenger seat was a woman who turned out to be a well-known local prostitute, Olivia Reivers. In the driver's seat was a thirty-four-year-old lorry driver from Bradford. His name was Peter William Sutcliffe. Olivia Reivers could count herself singularly fortunate that those officers arrived just when they did.

Under the media-inspired pseudonym of 'The Yorkshire Ripper', Sutcliffe had over the previous five years terrorized millions of women living in Yorkshire and Lancashire. During that period, no woman living in the two counties could leave their home alone without the spectre of his actions in their minds, fear in their hearts. Many years after it was all over, I was asked by the press for my retrospective thoughts. I said: 'The saga of the Yorkshire Ripper will no doubt continue over the years to excite question and comment. After all, in my experience, it remains unique in criminal annals, not just for its wickedness, but for its impact – great or small – on the very many who lived through those days and years.'

A combination of luck and prolonged investigative incompetence had left Peter Sutcliffe at liberty to commit at least thirteen murders of women, and seven attempted murders. Some of the victims were prostitutes; others were not. (I say 'at least' because senior officers always believed there were many more.) Those who died were usually rendered unconscious or worse by hammer blows to the head. Thereafter, many were subjected to truly appalling injuries to the abdomen and genitalia.

Of course, the identity of the man he was questioning was not known to Sergeant Ring at the time. However, a check quickly revealed that the car had false number plates, and that the driver's account that the woman was his girl-friend was a lie. He was taken into custody, but before he got into the police car he said that he was 'busting for a pee', and was allowed to go nearby for that purpose. Then he was taken to the local police station.

I will go on with the ensuing events of that night shortly, but first, you may well ask why had it taken five years to apprehend this man? At the time the crimes were committed, forensic scientific techniques were (by today's standards) limited. DNA was the tool of a far-distant future. The first use of computers to assist in criminal investigation would come only around 1986, with the introduction of HOLMES (the Home Office Large Major Enquiry System). Even then, HOLMES was unable to deal with separate, successive incidents. Serial crimes generated massive volumes of paper-work. The classifying and cross-referencing of thousands of statements and reports was frequently a futile exercise. Confusion was compounded by chaos.

In the Ripper case, the enquiry HQ was based at Millgarth police station in central Leeds. Now the site of a huge, ultra-modern shopping development, there was nothing ultra-modern about what went on at Millgarth during those five years. So many pieces of paper were generated that the upper floor set aside for the investigators could no longer safely contain the sheer weight of them. The flooring had to be specially reinforced.

Sutcliffe had some close shaves. In 1977 the police found on the body of a prostitute murdered by him in Lancashire a £5 note that was traced to the payroll of the haulage firm that employed him, but there the trail ended. Over the years he was questioned by police officers in a cursory fashion on some nine occasions. Quite remarkably, a friend of his, a man named Trevor Birdsall, had Sutcliffe as his companion in a car when on two occasions Sutcliffe got out of it in red light districts in Leeds, and spoke on his return of having attacked a prostitute (once with a stone wrapped in a sock). The second of these occasions transpired to be the first of the acknowledged attempted murders, on a prostitute called Olive Smelt, in the autumn of 1975. Birdsall, for whatever reason, said nothing until 1980, when he states that he went to the police.

The most glaring incident of what the Attorney-General was later to describe as Sutcliffe's charmed life occurred in August 1975 – before the first offence set out in the ultimate indictment. A teenager named Tracey Browne was attacked at night in a Yorkshire village. The man engaged her in conversation, and then struck her several hammer blows to the head. Her assailant only desisted and ran off when disturbed by the headlights of a passing car. Brain surgery saved his victim's life. Subsequently, she assisted in the preparation of a photofit image of the man who had attacked her. It bears an uncanny resemblance to Peter Sutcliffe. She also recalled that the man had a squeaky voice and a Yorkshire accent. Tracey Browne noted that subsequent photofits prepared by others who had survived attacks by Sutcliffe tallied with her own.

All this she disclosed to the police. Nothing came of this trail of clues. Even acknowledging the attractions of hindsight, the fact that these matters led nowhere surely calls into question the quality of the investigation.

But if we seek what in my opinion is the most likely explanation why the trails ultimately led nowhere, there can be little doubt that this man owed his protracted opportunities to kill to a fixation in the mind of the assistant chief constable of West Yorkshire Police, the late George Oldfield.

Mr Oldfield took charge of the case after understandable and growing concern about the failure of the police to make an arrest. Between March 1978 and March 1979 three letters were sent from the north-east of England – two to Mr Oldfield and one to the *Daily Mirror* newspaper. Each purported to come from the Ripper.

Notoriously, the assistant chief constable also received an audio tape. It was prefaced by the greeting 'I'm Jack'. Like the letters, it taunted Oldfield for his failure to make an arrest. Importantly, the accent of the male voice on the tape was assessed by experts. They concluded (correctly, as it turned out) that the author of the tape was from Wearside (Sunderland). I still have a newspaper photograph of Oldfield crouched attentively over a machine playing the tape, as if to say 'I'm on to you.'

But he was quite wrong. The letters and the tape formed a wicked hoax perpetrated by a Sunderland man named John Humble, then in his early twenties. Nearly thirty years later a cold case review, using DNA to test one of the envelopes sent by him, identified him as the hoaxer. In 2006 he was sentenced to eight years' imprisonment for perverting the course of justice.

Mr Oldfield disagreed with some of his officers who had misgivings about the authenticity of the material. After all, a study of criminology reveals numerous examples of misfits who latch on to high-profile investigations by falsely claiming involvement in the crimes committed. But Oldfield was adamant that the man that they were looking for came from the Sunderland area, and 40,000 men in that area were interviewed. Anything that pointed to a possible different conclusion – that the author of the 'I'm Jack' tape was *not* the Ripper – was flattened under the Oldfield steamroller.

———·•·———

In fact, Sutcliffe was a Yorkshireman. And I have recently looked again at a grainy video of the press conference held by the West Yorkshire Police after Sutcliffe's arrest.

There is the chief constable, Ronald Gregory, scarcely suppressing a grin as he speaks to the assembled throng of journalists. On his immediate right sits George Oldfield, with a broad smile on his face. I am the first to agree with the saying that the man who never makes a mistake never makes anything. I also respect the fact that Mr Oldfield can no longer answer for himself. But I also think of the two women murdered in 1979, and the two in 1980 (along with two attempted killings in that year). I recall the mother of the final victim, Jacqueline

Hill, seeking public vindication by way of court action against the police for what she described as their negligence in failing to identify Sutcliffe much earlier. I cannot for the life of me see what Mr Oldfield had to smile about. The whole investigation came to be widely regarded as a woeful catalogue of sustained incompetence, a conclusion endorsed in 1986 by the findings of a wide-ranging inquiry conducted by Sir Lawrence Byford, then HM Chief Inspector of Constabulary.

———

Back (or rather, forward) now to Sutcliffe's arrest in Sheffield. Having arrived in the police station, he again asked to use the lavatory. (Plainly, he had a limited imagination when seeking pretexts for being out of sight of the police.) After he emerged, a prescient policeman looked in the lavatory cistern. In it he found a knife.

It began to dawn on the officers that here – by sheer chance – they might have in their custody the serial killer who had been the subject of a manhunt for five years. As attention increasingly focused on Sutcliffe, Sergeant Ring (the arresting officer) had a sudden thought. He drove back to where he had made the arrest. In the area where Sutcliffe had 'gone for a pee' he recovered a knife and a ball-pein hammer (a hammer with one of its two heads rounded, a tool used by sheet metal workers).

The police knew that a trademark of the Ripper murders, according to the pathologists, was that just such a weapon was used to disable the victims, if not to kill them. Sutcliffe had been arrested when accompanied by a prostitute. The inference was obvious and compelling. He was questioned on that basis. After some period of questioning in Sheffield, a Detective Inspector Boyle said to him, 'I think you are in serious trouble.' There followed the following exchange:

SUTCLIFFE: I think you have been leading up to it.
BOYLE: Leading up to what?
SUTCLIFFE: The Yorkshire Ripper.
BOYLE: What about the Yorkshire Ripper?
SUTCLIFFE: Well, it's me. I'm glad it's all over.

Isn't it truly ironic that years of investigation by hundreds of police officers had come to nothing? Then along comes Robert Ring – 'Sergeant Plod', a twenty-six-year police service veteran, no doubt nearing retirement. Doing no more than his humdrum duty and then acting on a hunch. ('Just old-fashioned coppering', he was later to say of his actions.) To him, it seems to me, is owed credit for the arrest of perhaps the most wanted criminal in England during the last century.

Sutcliffe made a statement under caution admitting the crimes for which he was later indicted. The statement took sixteen hours to dictate. Two matters about its content are worthy of note. First, nowhere in it did he make any mention of hearing voices from God, a claim which was to feature so prominently at a later stage. Second, the police always believed that the murders and attempted murders that he admitted at that time were by no means a comprehensive catalogue. There remains the conviction that he was responsible for many more. Some time later, the then assistant chief constable of West Yorkshire, Keith Hellawell, reopened the investigation and reached the careful conclusion that ten other killings were probably attributable to Sutcliffe. He sought to put them to the man, but was met with a refusal to answer any questions. In this context, it is interesting to note that as far back as 1969 (six years before the date of the first offence set out in the indictment), Sutcliffe was arrested at night in possession of a hammer, and was convicted of the offence of going equipped for theft.

News of the arrest spread like wildfire. My wife said that she felt very sorry for whoever had to defend him. When I replied that it could be me, she teasingly said that it would mean divorce! She need not have been concerned. Within two days of the arrest, my clerk telephoned me to say that the office of the Director of Public Prosecutions wished to retain me to lead for the prosecution. Matrimonial harmony was restored.

Between the time of his arrest in Sheffield on 4 January 1981 and that of his trial in May, Sutcliffe was detained at Armley Prison in Leeds. During that period, two episodes were the harbingers of issues that were to dominate the trial.

On 8 January Sonia Sutcliffe visited her husband. A prison officer named Leach was present throughout the visit. Sutcliffe told her that he had given the police details of all that he had done. He said that he expected to get thirty years in prison. (That was, as it turned out, precisely the minimum period of detention specified by Mr Justice Boreham when passing sentence.) But, he said to his wife, 'if he could make people believe that he was mad, he would only do ten years in the loony bin'. It is interesting to record that at his trial Sutcliffe agreed in evidence that he had said 'something like that'. On 14 April, Sutcliffe insisted to a prison officer escorting him from Leeds to the Old Bailey, to which the trial had been transferred, that he was 'normal', and was apparently greatly amused that the doctors considered him to be disturbed.

Other events preceding the trial took a highly unusual course. I had been instructed to lead John Hitchen, a very experienced Leeds-based barrister with an extensive junior practice. In those days (and for all I know, even now) it was the historic right of the Attorney-General of the day to intervene, that is, to take over the leading role in a prosecution team, leaving the QC and junior as his subordinates in the conduct of the case.

At this time, the Attorney-General was Sir Michael Havers (his father had been a High Court Judge; his younger son became a QC, and his older son, actor Nigel, is renowned still for his part in *Chariots of Fire*, as well as for many other film and TV performances). He intervened. Despite my personal disappointment, I could not blame him for wanting a major slice of the action. After all, he was a politician as well as a lawyer. No doubt, the prospect of being the prosecutor in such a very high-profile case was irresistible to him.

The trial was transferred to the Central Criminal Court in London – the Old Bailey. Plainly, it could not be held in the north, for the risk of jury bias was patent and overwhelming. The judge was Mr Justice Boreham, a very experienced and able High Court Judge. I had appeared before him many times when he was for some years a presiding judge of the North-Eastern Circuit. The scene was set for the trial, to be held in May 1981.

Its commencement was marked by unprecedented media coverage. Press tickets were at a huge premium on the black market. It was dubbed 'The trial of the century'.

A word about the medico-legal background to the trial. By virtue of the Homicide Act of 1957, English criminal law affords a special defence to a person charged with murder. It is called 'diminished responsibility'. In lay terms, it allows a defendant to assert that although as a matter of fact he or she was responsible for the death, his or her mental state was such at the time of their actions as substantially to diminish their responsibility for what they did. (I should add that this provision does not afford a defence to someone whose conduct is simply the product of a psychopathic personality disorder.) The burden of establishing that this is (probably) the case rests on the defence. If they discharge that burden, then the verdict is one of not guilty of murder, but guilty of the lesser offence of manslaughter. This special defence applies only to murder, not to attempted murder.

The indictment alleged thirteen counts of murder, and seven of attempted murder. At a very early stage James Chadwin QC (for Sutcliffe) indicated that his client would be pleading guilty to the seven charges of attempted murder. As for the thirteen counts alleging murder, he would offer pleas of not guilty, but guilty to manslaughter on the basis of diminished responsibility. If, then, there was to be any issue for trial by a jury on the pleas offered, it would be a medical one. The decision would rest almost entirely on psychiatric opinion as to Sutcliffe's mental state at the material times, and its relevance to the thirteen fatal attacks.

To that end, four forensic psychiatrists had examined Sutcliffe, each visiting him in custody on a number of occasions. When I say 'examined' in the context of their diagnoses, it meant close questioning both as to what he had done *and* why he had done it. Two of the doctors were instructed by the prosecution; two by the defence. All four prepared reports for the assistance of the court and of counsel. (Prosecution and defence reports were exchanged.)

Their conclusion was unanimous. Sutcliffe was at all material times suffering from paranoid schizophrenia – a condition which accounted for his conduct, and the nature of which substantially diminished his responsibility within the meaning of the law. That is to say, it was their opinion that his ability to understand his conduct or to form a rational judgement as to what he was doing was substantially impaired.

The exclusive basis for this conclusion rested in all four instances on what Sutcliffe had told them. He said that while working as a gravedigger in a churchyard he had heard a voice from God that commanded him to kill prostitutes. This was referred to throughout the trial that was to follow as his 'divine mission'. That (he told the doctors) was the sole prompting for what he had done. In particular, he denied that his conduct contained any perverted sexual element. He was God's instrument – neither more nor less.

Here came the crunch. Sir Michael decided that in the light of the expert consensus the prosecution should accept the pleas to guilty of manslaughter, not murder. He would invite the judge to dispose of the case accordingly. No jury would be involved.

John Hitchen and I did not agree with this, and made our view plain to the Attorney-General. First, having regard to the wholly exceptional gravity of the case, it was our view that the public interest in seeing justice done in an open trial was overwhelming. This was not a situation the outcome of which should be seen as the product of a 'carve-up' between the lawyers. Too many people's lives had been affected by these events for far too long for them to be content with such a cosy disposal.

Crucially, I myself was entirely satisfied that the divine mission as the foundation for the diagnosis did not bear the detailed scrutiny that it should receive if subject to careful cross-examination. I was confident that the circumstances of each killing revealed the inherent falsehood of Sutcliffe's account to the doctors. For example, there was no doubt not only that some of the victims were not prostitutes, but that they could not possibly have been thought to be such by anybody – even this man. Tellingly (to my mind), the nature of some of the terrible injuries inflicted on his victims raised the compelling inference that there was a perverted sexual element in the mind of the assailant. I strongly held the view that the divine mission could be exposed as a pack of lies. Sutcliffe had duped the doctors into their diagnosis.

I vividly remember a gathering at the Attorney-General's chambers in the Courts of Justice in the Strand. Its purpose was to meet the two psychiatrists instructed by the prosecution and to test out the soundness of their diagnosis. Sir Michael courteously invited Hitchen and me to ask some questions. After it was all over, one of the senior detectives in the case told us that one of the doctors had said to him ruefully that they thought Sir Michael was a gentleman – but they did not much care for the 'two gorillas he had brought down from the North'.

Well, despite our explicit reservations, the Attorney-General decided that on the day appointed for the judge to give directions as to the future conduct of the trial he would stick to his decision. He would submit to Mr Justice Boreham that, in the light of the unanimous psychiatric opinion, the prosecution were minded to dispose of the case then and there by way of pleas of guilty to manslaughter, not murder.

In fairness to Sir Michael, I have no doubt that in this case he felt it was a distinction without any practical difference. Sutcliffe was going to be detained for a very long time indeed, if not for ever, whether in a prison or a secure hospital. Either way, the public would be safe from him. And I suppose, too, that the thought might have crossed his mind that nobody in their right mind could have been so depraved. ('He must have been mad . . .') To my mind, such considerations were wholly wide of the mark.

As it turned out, that was also the clear view of the judge. Normally, if the prosecution decide that they are willing to allow a case to be dealt with on the basis of a lesser offence, then the tribunal will not demur. It happens often, up and down the land. But there can be no doubt that any judge has the right to question the position, and to invite the prosecution to think again. That is precisely what happened on the morning appointed for the directions hearing in the

case of R v Peter William Sutcliffe in No. 1 Court at the
Old Bailey. As I have said, this was the occasion for directions
to be given as to the future conduct of the case. First and
foremost, it was the time for the Attorney-General to advise
the court of his conclusions, and to give his reasons in
support of them.

In the light of what followed, there was a deal of ill-
informed speculation as to why it happened. Leslie Boreham
and Michael Havers had been long-time sparring partners
as Silks on the South-Eastern Circuit. It was said that there
was little love lost between them. The judge was the son of
a policeman who became assistant chief constable of Suffolk.
Much of his time at the Bar had been spent as a prosecutor.
Did these factors sway him? I do not accept for one moment
that this speculation was well-founded. Leslie Boreham was
a stern but very fair man, and vastly experienced.

In some two hours of exchanges between the Attorney-
General and the judge, it became increasingly apparent to
me that the latter was deeply dissatisfied with the prospect
that the case should be disposed of on the basis of the offered
pleas. (At one stage, Sir Michael whispered to me that he
believed that the Judge was with him, but that he was putting
on a very good show for public consumption. My reply was
that if indeed it was no more than 'a good show', the judge
was a fine thespian.) Mr Justice Boreham had sat in Yorkshire
countless times as a presiding judge. He was well aware of
the impact of Sutcliffe's reign of terror upon the population
at large – and upon women in particular.

At the conclusion of submissions, Sir Michael was told by
the judge of his deepest misgivings as to the proposed course.
It was the judge's view that the issue was pre-eminently one
for a jury to decide, notwithstanding the consensus of the
psychiatric opinion. He was firmly opposed to the prospect
of what the public might view as a private deal between the

lawyers and the doctors. The Attorney-General was asked to think again.

This placed Sir Michael in a very difficult situation, even though it was one entirely of his own making. First, there could be no doubt that, despite his status as Attorney-General, the prosecution would have to accept that the matter should now proceed as a trial by jury on the issue of Sutcliffe's mental state. But he had publicly gone to great lengths to assert that he personally was content to abide by the psychiatric opinion. If he was now to yield to the judge's view that this was a matter for a jury, then how could he rationally be seen to challenge the evidence that he had specifically acknowledged as being reliable, and that he wished to rely upon? It was perfectly obvious to all of us that he could not put himself in that position.

In those circumstances, Sir Michael concluded that whilst he would still cross-examine Sutcliffe, should he give evidence, the central task of cross-examining the defence psychiatrists would have to be undertaken by me, not him. By this very unusual route, the 'gorillas from the North' had their way.

I had some weeks to prepare my cross-examination. I rented a service flat in London and knuckled down. (Apart from the scale of the task, I remember my stay in that flat for a quite separate reason. One morning, I went to collect the milk bottle from the front doorstep. The door swung closed and locked me out. I had no key. Dressed only in my underpants, I had to cross the Brompton Road and make a reverse-charge call to Chelsea police station. I can tell you that the officers who attended took some persuading that I was a QC preparing my cross-examination in the Sutcliffe trial.)

My central purpose was to construct a detailed analysis of the nature of the killings and their surrounding circumstances. By this means I intended to show clearly that there was no 'divine mission' to kill prostitutes. If the defence failed to establish as much, then since the diagnosis of paranoid schizophrenia rested solely on that premise, the doctors had been duped. The verdicts on the murder charges had to be 'guilty'.

But before that stage was reached it was for the Attorney-General to open the case for the Crown. Towards its conclusion, he said to the jury, 'You will have to decide whether, as a clever, callous murderer he has set out to provide a cock and bull story to avoid conviction of murder.'

Sutcliffe gave evidence. Slight of build, mild in manner, he was also plainly intelligent – and articulate. He spoke of his delusions as to the mission to kill prostitutes. He was cross-examined by Sir Michael. I mean no disrespect whatever to the Attorney-General, a charming, intelligent and highly experienced advocate, when I offer the following assessment of their exchanges. They struck me not so much as a confrontation between the senior law officer of the Crown and the (then) most prolific killer of our lifetimes, but more as a civilized dialogue at an academic level between equals. How well do I remember the moment when Sir Michael put a certain proposition to Sutcliffe, only to receive the reply, 'Fine words Mr Attorney – but well wide of the mark.' The indelible impression with which I was left was that his appearance in the witness box was Sutcliffe's last chance to strut a stage invested with the colossal notoriety of the forensic spotlight – and he enjoyed every minute of it.

I hope that I do Sir Michael no posthumous injustice when I confine myself to saying that the exchanges between him and the accused did little to throw light on the issue for the jury. All of us who were involved recognized that it was the doctors' evidence that must be the focus. And so it was down to me.

The principal diagnostician called by the defence was Dr Hugo Milne, a distinguished forensic psychiatrist from Leeds of some thirty years' experience, and Sutcliffe's chief examiner. I had encountered him professionally many times, and his evidence was at the very forefront of the diagnosis: I knew that all the other psychiatrists who had examined Sutcliffe in prison had essentially designated him to be the front-runner. Knowing therefore that my cross-examination of him was the key to the outcome of the case, I maintained a sustained and detailed challenge of his opinion over a period of many hours.

As a very young man at the Bar, I remember being led by a distinguished QC, who once said to me of the art of cross-examination, 'If you can't poison the atmosphere in the first ten minutes, then sit down.' Mindful of this, I spent literally hours of my preparation on what should be my first question of Dr Milne. In the event, it was: 'Of everything that Sutcliffe told you about his reasons for killing these women, was there any single thing that you did not accept?' Truly, Morton's Fork. If the doctor said that he had indeed accepted everything, then I knew that I could demonstrate that on the evidence the 'divine mission' was patently false. If, on the other hand, he was to acknowledge that there were parts of what he was told about which he had reservations, then it was a recognition that he might have been deliberately deceived.

Dr Milne chose to say that he accepted everything the accused had told him about the promptings for his conduct. Hence came the launch pad for my cross-examination. It lasted some hours, going into a second day. Some have said that the very profession of forensic psychiatry was on trial in that courtroom. I am also told that transcripts of my challenge to Dr Milne still surface amongst the members of the Bar as a model of the art of cross-examination. If that is so, I became an unwitting instructor. Whether my challenge was worth studying, I do not know. What I did was a creature of a time and a place, and it served its purpose.

In my prologue to this memoir, I cautioned myself against the temptations of egotism. I hope that in recording some of the exchanges between myself and Dr Milne may be found the essential key to the verdicts of the jury. I set them out for that reason, and for no other.

Hugo Milne was well known to me, and I liked and respected him in equal measure. But in this case, I was confident that he (and the other forensic psychiatrists) had got it all wrong. He had interviewed Sutcliffe on eleven occasions in total. Only during the eighth of those – two months after his arrest – did Sutcliffe first mention to the doctor the so called 'divine mission'.

Dr Milne's report included a number of observations. First, that he was on the lookout for any attempt to simulate mental illness, but found no evidence of it at all. Second (and most tellingly), 'I am convinced that the killings were not sexual in any way, and that the stabbings . . . had no sexual component.' He also said that he could find no reason why Sutcliffe had repeatedly stabbed some of his victims through the same entry wound. To the doctor's mind, this did not demonstrate any 'sexual symbolism'.

And so it will be obvious that the issue of divine mission on the one hand, or deception of the doctors by a clever sexual deviant on the other, was the stark choice. Was the certainty of Dr Milne (and others) that the killings were not sexual in any way a well-founded one, or had they all been duped? It was to that conflict that I directed my cross-examination.

I have already spoken of the length of my cross-examination. I hope that the few excerpts that follow will sufficiently show how it went. (I do not always quote the reply; the sting often lies in the form of the question.)

HO: Over half of the attacks took place on Friday or
        Saturday nights, when his wife was at work. If
        Sutcliffe was no more than the helpless and hapless
        victim of God's will, why did God confine himself
        so much to those two evenings, when his wife was
        away at work?

HO: During the overall period of years we are looking
        at, there was a year when Sutcliffe was away in
        London, attacked nobody during that time, as far
        as we know. Is this God only a Yorkshire God?

Dr Milne gave evidence that some paranoid schizophrenics
are 'extremely cunning, premeditative in their actions, and
determined not to be found out'.

HO: That is surely the hallmark of many normal
        criminals. How does that further your diagnosis,
        doctor?

Milne's attention was then drawn to three murders: those
of Elena Rytka (1978), Josephine Whittaker (1979) and
Marguerite Walls (1980):

HO: I suggest that certainly in those three cases,
           there was a sexual element in the mind of the
           assailant.
DOCTOR: That may be.

I particularly asked him to consider the death of one of
these women. In the course of killing her, he had used a
long, specially sharpened screwdriver which he inserted
repeatedly in and out of the vagina:

HO: Looking at that evidence, your opinion that there was no sexual element does not appear to be right, does it, doctor?

DOCTOR: No.

HO: Why do you suggest that Sutcliffe was reluctant to acknowledge this specific grotesque conduct with the screwdriver?

DOCTOR: Because of what people might think of him. (Gasps from public gallery)

HO: Is that a seriously considered answer? That this man who had admitted thirteen killings and seven attempted killings was concerned that people might feel even more hostile to him if he admitted his use of the screwdriver? I put it to you, Dr Milne, that this man was not a tortured soul, being told by God 'you must kill'. He is a man who craves for it, like an addict for their next shot of heroin.

DOCTOR: He never, ever wanted to be seen as a sexual killer.

HO: No because if he puts himself forward as a sexual killer, then the divine mission goes out of the window. That's why, isn't it, doctor?

DOCTOR: It could be.

And finally:

HO: If the jury decide that Sutcliffe knew full well that his last six victims were not prostitutes, then the divine mission to kill prostitutes lies in smithereens?

DOCTOR: I agree.

HO: Then it becomes murder?

DOCTOR: Yes.

Dr McCullough was the director of the Park Lane Special Hospital in Liverpool. He had also interviewed Sutcliffe, and he gave evidence confirming Dr Milne's diagnosis. When I asked him at what point he had first troubled to look at the prosecution evidence in the case, he gave the remarkable reply that he only saw it the day before the trial began, and therefore, of course, he was wholly unaware of the details of what Sutcliffe had inflicted on his victims before he made his diagnosis. At that juncture, he readily agreed with the judge's intervention, namely that actions speak louder than words. Nor, he acknowledged, had he spoken to any of the accused's family, friends or workmates. It seemed to me that those concessions served to render his diagnosis worthless. I did not cross-examine him for much longer.

Dr Kay was a psychiatrist instructed by the prosecution, but called by the defence. I do not recall his testimony being treated by either side as further illuminating the issue.

So much, then, for the evidence given at the trial that was directed to assisting the jury to answer the jackpot question of Sutcliffe's promptings for his conduct. I must now tell you of a piece of evidence that was *not* put before the jury and which, astonishingly, remained unknown to any of the prosecution team at any material time. Indeed, its existence only emerged over twenty years after the trial.

When Sutcliffe was arrested in Sheffield, he was strip-searched at the police station. According to a detective concerned in the investigation, he was wearing trousers, but beneath them no underpants. He had them in a pocket. According to the officer's account (later to be broadcast in a documentary), beneath his trousers he was wearing a green-coloured pair of loose-fitting tights. The crotch area had been cut away, and at knee level both legs were padded. (I have seen a photograph of them.) This bizarre attire surely spoke in the most deafening terms of the wearer's purpose.

As the same detective was to say many years after the event, it was obvious that after the wearer had felled (if not killed) his victim he would kneel over the torso (or corpse) and 'pleasure himself'.

If that account is to be accepted, and *if* the photograph is indeed of tights being worn by Sutcliffe at the time of his arrest, where are we? I am not naïve enough to conclude that the photograph I have seen proves anything of itself. (I remind myself of the man who said that he had swum the English Channel, and took his hearer to the cliffs of Dover to see the Channel in order to prove it.) But if the account given is reliable, then it is totally impossible to comprehend a piece of evidence more utterly damning to the suggestion of divine mission than that garment and the circumstances of its discovery. Yet it remained a secret. At whose instance? For what conceivable purpose? Where, and in what circumstances, did the photograph first see light? Why did any of those who first saw the garment remain silent? What prompted this revelation so many years later? By whom was it first publicly revealed, and to whom? I can answer none of those questions. What I can venture to suggest is that, had this been part of the picture in those early months of 1981, it is doubtful if there would have been a trial of a medical issue at all. It is certainly the most extraordinary occurrence of the many that have featured in my professional lifetime.

Well, the jury reached their verdicts. The foreman's answer of 'Guilty' in response to the question as to their verdict on count one (murder) inevitably signified that the verdict on the other twelve counts would be the same. My junior said behind me in a scarcely suppressed stage whisper, 'Bingo!'

The judge sentenced Sutcliffe to life imprisonment, accompanied by a recommendation that he serve no less than thirty years – with a rider that he hoped that in this case 'life' would mean just that. Peter William Sutcliffe then disappeared from our view down the dock steps of No. 1 Court at the Old Bailey. I know that I am very far from alone in seeing him then as the same enigmatic figure that he had been when arraigned.

———

Subsequent events took a curious turn, and an ironic one. Despite the jury's rejection of the diagnosis of psychiatric illness, the prison medical service concluded that Sutcliffe was indeed a paranoid schizophrenic, and in 1984 he was transferred from Parkhurst maximum security prison to Broadmoor Hospital. (No doubt the late Attorney-General would be heard to say 'I told you so', but then the opinions on which that decision rested were not subject to the close scrutiny and challenge that the original ones had received in No. 1 Court at the Old Bailey in 1981.) Years later, in 1993, he began a course of treatment with anti-psychotic drugs, and twenty years on, the doctors concluded that his condition had been contained. By then it might well have been a different generation of psychiatrists who conducted the reassessment. I strongly suspect that in this case a definitive diagnosis will always prove an elusive target for the forensic psychiatrists. In any event, in 2016 Sutcliffe was transferred back into a prison environment. In 2010, under more recent legislation, it had already been judicially decided that he should be the subject of a 'whole life' sentence. It is singularly unlikely, in my opinion, that he will ever be released.

There was another sad postscript to the trial (and one to which I have already briefly alluded). Sutcliffe's last victim was a twenty-year-old university student, Jacqueline Hill, murdered in Headingley, Leeds in November 1980. Her mother was understandably incensed and deeply distressed at the failure of the West Yorkshire Police to identify Sutcliffe long before he had the opportunity to commit his later killings. I was asked whether I would act for her in her proposed claim for damages against the police. Having regard to my former position as a prosecutor in the case, it would have been improper for me to do so. She went elsewhere. Unfortunately, it was ultimately concluded that in law she had no cause of action.

All but two of the professional actors in that drama are now gone from us. The judge, the Attorney-General, John Hitchen and Jim Chadwin are no more. I am sure that for each of them, as it still is for me, the trial was a memory that never left them.

That is enough of Peter William Sutcliffe. I don't doubt that my part in his trial will surface in my obituary, and I could wish for nothing more than that it might afford a suitable epitaph for my life as an advocate at the English Bar.

———

As it turned out, 1981 was an exceptional year for me in the context of homicide. In just two cases I had to address a total of thirty-nine unlawful deaths. Sutcliffe accounted for thirteen of them; the remainder involved a nineteen-year-old man named Peter Lee.

BRUCE GEORGE PETER LEE

Fire-raiser or fantasist?

I was instructed to defend Peter Lee (as he was usually identified), the child of a prostitute who never knew his father. He was a pitiful figure, a spastic-hemiplegic who suffered from epilepsy. In the area of Kingston-upon-Hull where he lived he was known to all the locals as 'Daft Peter'. Lee's only claim to fame (if it can be so described) was that by virtue of the events that brought him to my door he would be recorded as the perpetrator of, at that time, the largest number of homicides ever set out in one indictment.

Over a period of five years between 1972 and 1979, a number of fires had occurred in Hull. Some involved ordinary dwellings. In those instances, a total of fifteen people, young and old, died. A separate episode involved a fire at a residential home for elderly men in which no less than eleven residents died. In all but one case, the fires were for a long time treated as accidental.

The last fire was in December 1979 and caused the death of three youngsters. Lee was one of many questioned by the police as a possible suspect, and he admitted that he was the arsonist. In the course of further questioning, and to the complete surprise of the police, he went on to admit being the author of nine other fires in Hull over the previous seven years, including the fire at the residential home.

As I have already said, all the fires save the last had been treated as accidental. Inquests had been conducted and in each case verdicts of misadventure entered by the coroner. In particular, at the inquest concerning the deaths at the residential home, evidence had been given by a Home Office expert that it was likely the fire had started accidentally as a result of a blow lamp being used by a plumber working on the premises at the time. Remarkably (to my mind), when Lee's confession to deliberately setting fire to the place emerged, the expert began dancing to a different tune. He then gave as his opinion that Lee's confession of deliberate arson was in fact consistent with his (the expert's) findings.

Bearing in mind this history, and Peter Lee's obvious mental frailty, Detective Superintendent Sagar, who was in charge of the case, viewed Lee's admissions with some scepticism. Sensibly, he decided to test them out. Lee took the police on a tour of the sites of the various fires and confirmed his responsibility for them. The police then deliberately took him to the scene of a fire where an arsonist had already admitted his guilt and had been dealt with by the court. They were anxious to test the reliability of Lee's confessions by seeing whether he would 'admit' that he was the arsonist in that case as well. Lee denied it, saying that he'd never been there. This confirmed in the mind of his interrogators that his admissions to causing the other fires were not simply the product of fantasy, but were reliable and true.

Lee said that he was fascinated by fire and had given no thought to the potentially fatal consequences. Having regard to all the circumstances of the case, including the medical reports, the prosecution agreed to accept his pleas to manslaughter on the grounds of diminished responsibility. Before the day appointed for the hearing the judge (Mr Justice Tudor Evans) agreed that this was the appropriate disposal.

Despite all this, I continued to be deeply concerned that the intended pleas might be unreliable – that Lee was not the arsonist responsible for any of the fires. The judge undoubtedly had the power in these circumstances, if he shared my concern, to direct that simple pleas of 'not guilty' be entered in respect of all the charges, and to leave it to a jury to decide. For that reason, I applied to the judge to take that course. He declined to do so.

In January 1981 at Leeds Crown Court, Lee pleaded not guilty to twenty-six counts of murder but guilty in each case to manslaughter on the grounds of diminished responsibility. He also pleaded guilty to eleven counts of arson. An order was made that he be detained in a secure hospital without limit of time, unless and until he was deemed fit for release.

I persisted, arguing the matter in 1983 before the Court of Appeal. In the forefront of my submissions to the three judges was the fire at the residential home. The court granted my application that the Home Office 'expert' should attend to be cross-examined. I did so on the basis that his change of grounds, namely, from an accidental fire to deliberate arson, rendered his opinion worthless. I went on to argue from that premise that there was a 'domino effect' on the reliability of the confessions to the other fifteen deaths. My submission was that if the court concluded that his admission to setting fire to the residential home was unreliable, who was to say with confidence that any of the other admissions were worthy of credit?

The court did not agree. Lord Justice Ackner (later a Lord of Appeal) told me upon the court's return to give its judgement that he had some good news and some bad news for my client.

The court accepted that the expert's volte face rendered the convictions arising from the fire at the residential home unsafe. Most unusually, and despite Lee's pleas of guilty to the deaths, those eleven convictions were quashed. That outcome alone makes this case worthy of account.

That was the good news. However, the court was satisfied that the confessions to the remaining fifteen offences were the product of admissions freely and voluntarily given, and were reliable. That was the bad news.

I am certain that no other advocate has seen his client acquitted of eleven counts of homicide despite his guilty pleas. I am even more certain that none has left the court with his client still convicted of another fifteen identical offences. Lord Justice Ackner described the outcome for me as a 'pyrrhic victory'. I have always thought that to express it in that way was a considerable understatement!

There were two other interesting consequences of the case

of R v Bruce George Peter Lee. First, Superintendent Sagar sued the *Sunday Times* newspaper for libel in suggesting that he and his team might have misconducted themselves in the way that they secured Lee's confessions. The case was settled, no doubt in a way that reflected the view of the Court of Appeal that all the confessions were freely given and (with one exception) reliable. The second outcome is that I have reason to believe that more than thirty years later, the convictions have been the subject of an application to the Criminal Cases Review Commission to re-ventilate my arguments. I do not know the outcome. As far as I am aware, however, Peter Lee (now in his fifties) is still regarded as a danger to the public and remains in a secure place.

PAUL VICKERS AND PAMELA COLLISON

A rare case of poisoning

I was instructed in 1982 to prosecute Paul Vickers and Pamela Collison at Teesside Crown Court. Vickers was a surgeon, Collison his mistress. They were jointly charged with the murder of Vickers' wife. The case was unusual for a number of reasons – first, because it was a case (effectively) of murder by poison.

The prosecution alleged that the two accused had determined to free themselves of the restraint imposed by marriage on Mr Vickers. The evidence disclosed that over a substantial period of time, Vickers had deceived his wife into believing she was suffering from cancer. On that pretext, he had prescribed for her and administered to her a drug that ultimately had fatal consequences. It was alleged that Pamela Collison had not only collected the prescribed drugs from a chemist in Harley Street but had done so pursuant to the plan and knowing of their purpose. Vickers gave evidence on oath and was, accordingly, cross-examined by me.

A second unusual feature of the trial was that Pamela Collison chose (as she was fully entitled to do) not to give evidence. However, she also availed herself of the right then still available to an accused to make an 'unsworn statement from the dock'. She was also entitled to seek her counsel's advice on its form and content, and no doubt she did so.

In that statement, she denied any knowing involvement in unlawfully causing the death of Mrs Vickers. As I remember it, she cut an impressive figure as she stood in the dock making her statement. The judge properly reminded the jury that she had exercised no more than her right, but that the jury should be careful in deciding what weight they gave to it, bearing in mind that it was not being given on oath, and was therefore not subject to cross-examination.

Paul Vickers was convicted of murder and was sentenced to life imprisonment with a recommendation that he serve no less than thirty years. Pamela Collison was acquitted. In that same year, by Section 72 of the Criminal Justice Act of 1982, the right of an accused to make an unsworn statement from the dock was abolished. Thenceforth, an accused must either 'put up or shut up'.

In my latter years as a Silk my practice took on an overseas dimension. For that reason alone, my last two inclusions deserve to come from abroad.

In the spring of 1983 I was convalescing from a near-fatal bout of hepatitis when my clerk was asked if I would accept the brief to lead for the defence in a case in Zimbabwe in what was expected to be a long trial. Despite my condition, the temptation was irresistible. It proved a most formidable challenge. The nature of the case, my isolation so far from home, and the heat all combined to impose a huge burden. I was to find the whole experience the most demanding in my entire life at the Bar, and one during which I found it increasingly difficult to retain the necessary emotional detachment.

THE ZIMBABWE AIR FORCE SIX

Treason or torture?

On the night of 25 July 1982, saboteurs cut their way through the security fence surrounding Thornhill air force base in central Zimbabwe. They blew up thirteen aircraft, including twelve jet fighters. The damage was estimated at $7 million (the less tangible, but more significant cost to the air force lay in what followed, in terms of damage to morale, and the resignation of most of the officers who were essential to its continued operations). The security services in Zimbabwe suspected that the saboteurs were special agents who had infiltrated the country from South Africa.

Six air force officers were arrested. One of them, Air Vice Marshal Hugh Slatter, was on the brink of appointment as head of the air force. Philip Pile held the rank of Air Commodore. Of the remainder, two were wing commanders and two flight lieutenants. It was contended that each of them, acting together, was party to a conspiracy with authorities in South Africa to facilitate the sabotage.

For reasons that will soon become apparent, the firm of solicitors in Harare (formerly Salisbury) recognized that if the defence was to have any prospect at all of success, its key had to lie in a destructive cross-examination of the officers of the Zimbabwean security services. Their evidence as to confessions extracted from the accused men formed the exclusive basis for the case against them.

To that end, they first sought the services of Sydney Kentridge QC (and now also KCMG). Although this record is essentially autobiographical, he deserves more than just a bare mention of his name. He is certainly the most distinguished of South African-born advocates to have graced the English Bar in my lifetime. He and his wife were well known and admired as staunch opponents of apartheid.

Sydney Kentridge had achieved international fame in 1978, when acting as counsel for the family at an inquest in South Africa into the death of Steve Biko, a black activist who had died while in police custody. His performance on that occasion led Lord Alexander – himself an outstanding member of the English Bar – to applaud his 'remorseless and deadly cross-examination', by virtue of which 'he established that Biko had been killed by police brutality'. Clearly, the solicitors had fastened on absolutely the right man for the job. However, they were told that Kentridge had an existing and unbreakable professional commitment which meant that he could not accept the brief. The solicitors took stock. I remain exceptionally flattered that I became his substitute.

All the accused had made written confessions of their involvement in the acts of sabotage. As local criminal procedure required, they had additionally confirmed those confessions before a magistrate. If that evidence was proved to be reliable, then verdicts of guilty were inevitable. The crime alleged was akin to treason. The penalty was death.

The case for the defence was that in every instance the confessions and their subsequent adoption before a magistrate were false. They had been secured by torture, supported by deliberate, systematic, sustained and unlawful denial of access to the men's lawyers. The torture took the forms of electric shocks, beatings and persistent denial of sleep.

The trial lasted nine weeks, ending in late July 1978. No jury was involved. Presiding was Justice Enoch Dumbutshena, a black judge (later to become chief justice). He was assisted by two lay assessors, one a white man (a retired senior police officer) and the other a distinguished black, local official.

Initially, I stayed in Meikles, a luxury hotel in Harare. Later, I lived in a small rented house in the Harare suburbs. In both places, I suspected that my telephone was bugged. I was also advised by the office of the British High Commissioner that it was undesirable that my wife should join me at any time. Unsurprisingly, I did have the support of the already beleaguered whites in and around Harare. I was overwhelmed by offers of hospitality, which meant a good deal to me. However, I also have to say that the expectations of me they expressed added an increasingly anxious further burden as time went on.

As I have already suggested, it was crystal clear that the outcome of the trial would turn on the impact of cross-examination of the security officers who had obtained the written confessions. In the forefront of those witnesses was their man in charge, Chief Superintendent Muremba. It was crucial to our case that his testimony should be demolished. The ammunition I had came from many hours of preparation, greatly assisted by my junior, Ian Davidson, an able and industrious member of the local Bar. And so I set out to be a forensic bulldozer. It took many days as I faced Mr Muremba across that sweltering courtroom. (Imagine being be-wigged and gowned in a Turkish bath.) On the issue of the denial of access to the defendants' legal representatives, it was not solely a matter of word against word. We had prepared timetables in the form of charts, and these painted, I submitted, a trenchant picture of the constant transfer of all the men from one place to another just in time, over and over again, to frustrate the purpose of the imminent arrival of their lawyers.

I have warned myself previously of the dangers of egotism. It is particularly appropriate that I do so again now. But I do have the real comfort here of knowing that if I sound triumphal, my self-assessment enjoys the support of the trial's ultimate outcome. I believe that at the end of his time in the witness box, Mr Muremba left it a totally discredited witness. I was confident that, provided I was before a tribunal of independence and integrity, my clients were going to win the day. Despite that, I still recall myself as a physically and mentally exhausted figure going into the robing room and seeking reassurance from Ian Davidson.

'Well,' he said, 'you did miss one question.'

I could have killed him!

———

The record of the trial shows that in my closing submissions to the court I said the following: 'This trial has revealed abuse of the State's investigative processes on a grand scale . . . The conduct of the interrogators involved protracted and wholly unscrupulous violations of the defendants' legal rights, backed up in this court by dishonest evidence.' Thereafter, the trial was adjourned to a date in September, when the verdicts would be delivered.

August was a most anxious month. It seemed interminable to me. I flew out again to Harare in early September, and awoke very early on the day of the verdict. I took a long and lonely walk through the neighbouring streets, and then waited for a time outside the court building, beneath the jacaranda trees.

There was not an inch of spare room in the place when Justice Dumbutshena and his colleagues entered and sat down. Reading from a carefully written judgement, the court concluded that, by reason of what Americans would call abuse of process, the alleged confessions should be wholly disregarded. In the absence of any other incriminating evidence, all my clients were acquitted. My hope that I was before a tribunal of independence and integrity had been totally vindicated. There was this, too; I liked to think that Sydney Kentridge would share my overwhelming sense of relief. All six men were discharged from custody in appalling conditions in Chikurubi jail, where they had languished since their arrest.

Accompanied by many of their families and other supporters, we waited outside to greet my clients as men freed at last. We were to be disappointed in the most traumatic fashion. As soon as they had left the dock, 'the Air Force Six' were rearrested under emergency legislation and returned to prison.

Even now, as I recall those moments so many years ago, I cannot begin adequately to express my reaction. Outrage and a sense of total helplessness combined to leave me utterly despondent. All our endeavours, it seemed, had come to absolutely nothing. Providentially, however, help was at hand.

Robert Mugabe had only recently come to power. At that time, he was still anxious to maintain a civilized relationship with the UK. The Prince of Wales was due to visit Zimbabwe quite soon. It was 'made known' to the President that unless my clients were released and permitted to leave the country if they wished to do so, the royal visit would not take place. Second thoughts won the day. All the men were given their freedom. I don't know what life held for any of them afterwards, but I received their profound thanks. I still wish all of them and their families well.

I flew home via Johannesburg on a South African Airways flight. As we overflew Beit Bridge on the Limpopo River, which forms part of the frontier between Zimbabwe and South Africa, the captain of the aircraft told my fellow passengers that I was aboard. To my embarrassment, I was applauded.

A final word on my time in central Africa. I have spoken of the warmth of my welcome from white Zimbabweans. I want also to express my deep thanks to the black population that it was my good fortune to meet in that country. I met none from government circles, of course, but the ordinary folk I came across were invariably friendly, cheerful and keen to welcome me as a stranger in their land. I remain extremely grateful to them. When I read of what has happened to them and their country in the three decades that have since passed, I do so with infinite sadness.

———

Shortly after my return from Zimbabwe I was elected a Master of the Bench at Gray's Inn. Thus it was that I became 'Master Ognall' – the title by which I am still addressed when I am there, and one I had not enjoyed since I was an eight-year-old at Leeds Grammar School. What a very English quirk! To become what is called a Bencher is a privilege that I cherish. Sitting at high table in hall, I often think back to that November day in 1958 with the Treasurer of the Inn standing next to it as I approached him to be called to the Bar.

Although I didn't know it at the time, my practice as a member of the Bar was coming to an end. But before it was over, it took me to Hong Kong. Towards the end of 1984, the Attorney-General for Hong Kong, Michael Thomas QC, invited me there to lead a team in the preparation, committal for trial and prosecution of a number of defendants in a matter that became widely known as the Carrian Case (after a company said to be the primary vehicle for the fraud).

I spent many months in Hong Kong, and the place has exerted a fascination for me ever since. The Chinese who lived there were remarkable for their industry, their intelligence and their extraordinary sense of loyalty to their families in every generation. The non-Chinese (Gweilo, in Mandarin) population was a polyglot community from many countries and many different backgrounds. A good number came from the UK or the Commonwealth. A large proportion of them were refugees from one disappointment or another, including broken marriages. Many came from the professions. To me, in the main they were distinguished by ability, but sometimes also by an eccentricity that had not served them well in the country where they had started their careers. All had been tempted by a colony where earnings could be enormous and taxes were very low. Materialism was everywhere. As an Australian barrister who was a member of my team shrewdly noted, being in Hong Kong was like 'having Christmas every day'. He was absolutely right. I enjoyed the experience enormously, but there can be too much of a good thing. Even eccentricity can lose its charm.

In that context, and before I say any more about the case that took me there, I shall give you one example of the colourful canvas that Hong Kong has always been for me. The late Sir Denys Roberts, Chief Justice of Hong Kong, told me of a criminal appeal over which he had once presided. The appellant was represented by a well-known English-qualified barrister. As will become apparent, he was conspicuous for his (shall I say) unusual techniques in court. On this occasion, the appeal was, by a consent common to all but him, absolutely without merit. All three judges kept interrupting his submissions with forceful comments or questions that did not bode well for the outcome of the appeal.

The court rose for lunch, and on its return, counsel for the prosecution stood alone at the very large table below the bench on which counsel rested their papers. The Chief Justice asked him where his opponent was, since he must have known the time that the court was to resume?

With a degree of embarrassment, counsel pointed underneath the table. All three judges stood and peered over to have a view. Beneath the table was counsel for the appellant, apparently flicking a cigarette lighter on and off. 'Mr X. what on earth are you doing?' enquired Sir Denys. In sepulchral tones came back the muffled reply, 'Looking for justice, my lords.'

Despite the enchantments of the place, there was an ugly backdrop to the glittering façade of life in Hong Kong. It goes to explain what I have to say about the events that took me there. The ever-present awareness of money bred greed: those who had none were desperate to have some, while those who had plenty wanted even more. This was fertile ground for the seed of dishonesty. It was to be found at all levels of society – in the upper hierarchy of government, in trade and commerce, and among the professions. Its effect on many was gradual and insidious. It blunted true perception of what was acceptable conduct. Shady dealing became commonplace. Hitherto decent people knowingly and willingly accepted propositions that in a different milieu they would have instantly and firmly rejected. 'If they're all doing it, it must be OK' was the train of thought.

During my time there, ICAC, the government-established Independent Commission Against Corruption, had its own specially selected police team. They were always busy.

THE CARRIAN CASE

'In the teeth of the evidence . . .'

It began in this way. A major Malaysian bank suspected fraud in its Hong Kong subsidiary. It sent an internal auditor to investigate. Six months later, his body was found in a banana grove on the mainland of Hong Kong. He had been murdered. The subsequent police enquiries suggested a fraud of the dimensions of £250 million. Investors and creditors alike had been swindled. There was evidence implicating English-born solicitors and accountants, while the major Chinese involvement was said to be directed by two men – George Tan and Bentley Ho.

I led a team of three other barristers: John Sulan from Australia (later himself a judge in South Australia), Clive Grossman, originally a practitioner in Zimbabwe, and another Australian, a feisty young man named Mark Rice. Our initial task was to review the voluminous police material and to decide what offences had prima facie been committed, and by whom. (One very upsetting aspect of this undertaking was that in the light of our assessment, suspicion fell upon an English-born solicitor practising in Hong Kong, who committed suicide.) Once the charges and the identities of those to be charged had been determined, we moved forward to the committal proceedings before a magistrate. This is the process by which the prosecution call evidence designed to satisfy the court that each of the defendants has a case to answer. If so satisfied, the magistrate will commit the defendants to the High Court, to be tried by a judge and jury.

I, with my team, undertook the conduct of that preliminary hearing. It lasted many months, concluding at Easter 1985. Each defendant was represented by a QC from England. No stone was left unturned on their behalf. At the end of the day, the magistrate was satisfied that each defendant had a case to answer. Accordingly, he committed them to stand trial.

The trial date was some way off. Before it was reached, the Lord Chancellor, Lord Hailsham, asked me if I would accept appointment to the Queen's Bench Division of the High Court. I accepted, and so played no further part in what followed, but it bears record and certainly justifies the inclusion in this history.

Most unusually, a Judge of Appeal, Dennis Barker, was appointed to try the case. It is believed that he offered to take it on. There was much speculation at the time as to why. Although it was a very significant case, it was certainly within the competence of one of the first-instances judges of the High Court of Hong Kong (i.e. those judges who try the case with a jury, as opposed to judges of appeal). The prosecution evidence lasted well over a year. And here I come to another noteworthy feature of the case. At its conclusion, the judge ruled that none of the defendants had a case to answer. He directed the jury to acquit. The decision was greeted with astonishment in legal circles in the colony, including by me and my former team. It was reviewed on appeal, and was severely criticized by the court.

Dennis Barker never recovered from the censure; he soon retired to live in Cyprus. Four years later, aged sixty-three, he was killed in a collision between his car and a truck while driving down from the Trodos mountains. The circumstances of the accident remain uncertain. It was sadly typical of one facet of Hong Kong and the extremes that it generates that some time after his death, his penniless widow wrote to the *South China Morning Post* saying that she had sent his robes as a Judge of Appeal back to Hong Kong to be sold, in the hope that the sale would raise sufficient money for the purchase of a tombstone in the Cyprus graveyard, where his grave was otherwise unmarked.

And so, my days as a barrister and QC were at an end. I remember my last case very well. It was a relatively unimportant matter (except perhaps to my client), and I really had no merit on my side in the application I was making. My opponent was Alan Green QC, later to become Director of Public Prosecutions. There is no doubt that he was a most able and sometimes very funny advocate. He listened to my argument with palpable and growing astonishment. When his turn came to address the judge, he said that my submission reminded him very much of the trick performed by the Indian fakir using a magic carpet. By that, he said, he meant that it was obviously completely up in the air, and with no visible means of support. He was absolutely right!

Leaving the Bar undoubtedly occasioned very mixed feelings in me. But as a reputation in the profession is enhanced, counsel in question find themselves in the position of being asked to build more and more bricks with less and less straw. The burden grows with every passing brief. All that said, it remains for me to tell you that of all the days of my professional life, my twelve years as a Silk were beyond any shadow of a doubt professionally the happiest and most satisfying of all. It is in the nature of things that recollection fades. For me, those days never will.

4

ADVICE TO THE
YOUNG ADVOCATE

Before I turn to the last chapter of my professional life, I suppose this is the most suitable place for me to look back and answer a question that is frequently put to me even now. What are the essential qualities for jury advocacy? In seeking to answer that question, I look back over forty years of the law, as was said of Anthony Eden (who was driven from Number 10 after the debacle of the Suez crisis), as one who has a great future now long behind me.

I claim no monopoly of insight. I do not pretend to put the items that follow in any order of significance. But all are relevant.

Complete mastery of the facts and the relevant legal principles

This is not peculiar to jury advocacy in criminal courts, but a prerequisite of success in any field of legal practice. There is *no* escape from the hard work of preparation. I always tried to stand on my feet for the first time in any case believing that I knew as much and (hopefully) more about all its dimensions than anyone else involved in its preparation or conduct.

Against my own interest, I should say that there are still

occasions when, however rigorously you have mastered your brief, it can sometimes be the sudden thought or insight that comes in a flash that wins the day. In that context, I still remember a striking example.

I was instructed to lead a very experienced junior, John Mellor, in the defence at Bradford Crown Court of a wealthy scrap metal dealer accused of the knowing receipt of stolen goods on a very large scale. The case against him was formidable. The trial was estimated to last several days. The fees were generous, especially taking into account the fact that we were to be paid agreed 'refreshers' (as the profession describes them) for each day after the first that the case lasted. What I did not know was that John's fishing boat, the *Freda Mary*, which he kept at his holiday home in Skibereen in West Cork, was in need of a new inboard engine. Since the trial was inevitably going to run its course, John had ordered a new Perkins engine – to be funded out of the 'refreshers'. Alas!

As I was putting on my togs in the robing room on the first morning, it suddenly came to me from nowhere that there might – just might – be room, on some obscure basis that I can now no longer remember, for an application to the Circuit judge to stay the case. If the application were successful, the judge would stop the case there and then. Our client would be acquitted. There would be no trial.

It was a very long shot, but I gave it a go. To my surprise, and John Mellor's utter consternation, my submission was accepted by the judge, and our astonished client walked free. So much for the refreshers! My junior told me acidly that it was very unlikely that he would be asking for me to lead him in any other case.

In the end he relented, and indeed the very next summer, I went to West Cork and we went fishing for mackerel in the *Freda Mary*. I did not ask him how the inboard engine was going.

An extensive, but not ornate command of the English language is an obvious quality

I must agree that you either have this, or you don't.

An experience of life's realities, and especially its temptations

Leading to the ability to empathize with witnesses and jurors – and judges.

Independence of judgement and of conduct

Where circumstances demand it, no advocate should be afraid of standing up to a judge. Nor can there be any question of sycophancy towards those who instruct you – even though they are your paymasters. Equally, there can be no question of your simply doing your lay client's bidding if it conflicts with your professional duty. If you are a defender, that must not make you a mere 'mouthpiece'. One word perhaps sums all this up:

Integrity

On this matter, I am still often asked how I can reconcile the precept of integrity with defending an alleged criminal who I believe on the evidence (which is sometimes over-whelming) to be guilty.

This is my answer. Even if a client has admitted their guilt to you, you may still act within the bounds of your professional duty by testing the prosecution case as presented in the evidence that they call. But you may not in those circumstances call your client to give evidence. To do so would be a clear breach of your duty to the court. On the other hand, if your client denies the offence, then (whatever your own beliefs or misgivings) you must do your very best on their behalf. English criminal justice enjoins trial by jury – not trial by advocate. If counsel were to conduct themselves otherwise, then the fundamental right to legal representation as an essential part of the process of a fair trial would be rendered meaningless.

Flexibility – the capacity to think on your feet

The unforeseen – the unexpected – is a risk endemic in any evidence forming part of the trial procedure. The advocate must learn to adapt to meet the slings and arrows of outrageous fortune. Wherever possible, a virtue must be made out of the necessity they impose on the original strategy.

Relish the opportunity and the challenge

I cannot overstate this. Enjoyment of the task in hand. I was once astonished when talking about our lives with a QC who was a direct contemporary in the law. He confessed to me that each time he was about to go into court to embark upon a major trial he became physically sick. For me, he might as well have been speaking in a language wholly unknown to me. In all the major cases in which I became involved, adrenalin rode with me and was my welcome companion. When I knew that I was about to be called upon for the first time, my only thought was 'bring it on!'

The thespian within

This holds good even in these days when, to my mind, a featureless meritocracy seems to hold increasing sway.

I speak of the quality of a thespian as of being among the attributes of a successful jury advocate, but – like so many things in life – the advice is coupled with a caution. Insincerity will soon be twigged by most juries. They are not daft; they are quickly alert to the charlatan. There is a Latin maxim, '*Esse quam videri*' – to be, not just appear to be. Like so many of those ancient precepts, it still holds good.

'Off the cuff is out of bounds'

Always know what you intend to say, and have a reason for it. Do not be like the federal judge in the United States who was heard to observe, 'How do I know what I think, until I hear what I say?'

Self-awareness

A youngster who recognizes his or her weaknesses is an improver. Learn from your mistakes. Aldous Huxley said that experience is not what happens to you. It is what you *do* with what happens to you.

When I speak of learning from mistakes, your learning will be enhanced hugely if in the time you have out of court (and there will be quite a lot initially), you go and listen to the great and the good on their feet. Even they make mistakes, and so you will learn from them, as well as from your own experience, what to do – and what to avoid.

*Be aware of the danger of egotism. Do not confuse it
with self-confidence*

The boundary between the two is sometimes difficult to
discern. A story is told of the young composer who learned
of the death of Maestro Rossini at his home in France in
1868. Some little time later, he spoke to a much older
musician, and told him that he had composed a small piece
that he proposed to offer to be played at Rossini's memorial.
He asked his senior if he would listen to it and express his
opinion on the proposal. The piece was played. There
followed a long silence. 'Mm,' said the listener, 'on balance,
I think it would have been preferable if you had died, and
Rossini composed the music.'

Be brave

The intensely public media in which you will ply your trade
is not always an easy place A single mistake or misjudgement
can have momentous consequences for someone, or for many
people. But do not be overawed by consequences. Tread
carefully, but firmly.

*Once you have determined on your course, follow it
with confidence*

But do not confuse confidence with arrogance. General John
Sedgwick was a commander in the Union Army in the
American Civil War. At the Battle of the Wilderness in 1864
in Pennsylvania his troops were pinned down by Confederate
snipers. Despite this, he continued to place himself within

their lines of fire. When urged by some of his men to be more careful, he replied, 'Those devils couldn't shoot an elephant at this dist—'

Despite the formal and sombre character of the trial process, do remember that there are very few cases which do not admit of a humorous element

Sometimes humour may be introduced as a necessary means of alleviating for a short time the inevitable tensions attached to a particular case. All those involved in the situation, in whatever role they play, need a brief 'time out' to refresh the spirits. But sometimes the humour is designed for another purpose, and may be in the nature of a private joke between counsel. Looking far back, one such incident holds pride of place for me.

In the long, hot summer of 1976, I found myself involved in an extremely lengthy trial in Teesside concerning widespread corruption in the north-east of England. The facts do not matter. (Although it perhaps deserves mention that the proceedings were a spin-off from an earlier notorious case involving John Poulson, the corrupt architect from Pontefract whose tentacles embraced a large number of public figures including at least one of Cabinet rank.) The trial I am now mentioning did not even enjoy the redeeming feature of a high profile. Suffice it to say that in any competition for soporific impact, it would have walked away with first prize. Day after endless day we returned to our indifferent hotel in Middlesbrough, longing for a stiff drink, and consoled only by the fact that we were being paid for our suffering.

Out of this stygian gloom, a ray of light was offered to

us. I was one of a team of four prosecutors, second to Peter Taylor QC in the pecking order. One of our two juniors was a delightful fellow named Tony Purnell (who is sadly no longer with us). He came up with a splendid diversion. He devised a word game.

It took the form of four lists in which words of increasing difficulty were set out. List A contained words in most regular use; those in List B were slightly more obscure, and so on. You get the picture. The only common ground that all of them shared was that, on the face of it, all the listed words had absolutely nothing to do with bribery and corruption in County Durham.

The challenge to each of the eight QCs in the case was to employ at least one of the listed words in a question that they asked of a witness. If they did so, then all other counsel in the case would make a forfeit in coin of the realm, the amount depending on the status of the list from which the word had been extracted. List D was the premium list, entitling the orator who used any word in it to 50p from each of his colleagues. I remember that it included in a list devilishly designed to be wholly irrelevant to any issue in the trial the words 'cunnilingus' and 'rhododendron'.

Peter Taylor was not a whit deterred. The day this clandestine competition began, he was cross-examining one of the defendants, Alderman Andrew Cunningham. He invited the Alderman's attention to a book of photographs containing images of the home of the witness in Chester-le-Street.

'Please look at photograph 12. I believe that is a photograph of the window of your bedroom in that bungalow. It may not matter, but I think that we can all see that the view of it is partially obscured by a shrub – possibly [a

gasp from counsel's seats] – a rhododendron?' To the
judge's complete mystification, I was appointed ad hoc
treasurer as several pounds in 50p pieces was passed along
to me.

Never act as counsel for family or friends

I learned this principle the hard way – and it could have
been even worse. My client was a Lancashire haulier with
whom I shared a mutual friend. He was tried at the Old
Bailey for a fraud committed by his company on Common
Market funds. (Do I hear you say 'Not somebody else with
his nose in that trough?') As the trial proceeded, I began to
get cold feet. I became increasingly oppressed by the fear
that he might be convicted and (more importantly) receive
a prison sentence. In retrospect, my assessment of the situation was undoubtedly distorted by my tenuous friendship
with the defendant.

My cross-examination of the prosecution witnesses
had gone pretty well, but you never know. Un-
characteristically, I began to question myself as to the
prospects of success. However, I believed that if he changed
his pleas to 'guilty' this particular judge was likely to treat
that as sufficient mitigation to avoid the penalty of immediate imprisonment. I urged him to think about this change
of tack. He was initially obdurate in declining my advice,
but at the end of the following morning – before the
prosecution had concluded its evidence – he changed his
pleas as suggested. The judge said that after the lunch
adjournment he would hear my plea in mitigation and then
pass sentence.

As it so happened, during the short adjournment I

shared a lift with some of the members of the jury. Once my client had changed his pleas, they no longer had a part to play. To my complete dismay, one of them said to me, 'You could have knocked us over with a feather when your client admitted his guilt. We were all going to acquit him.'

I find it difficult to describe my feelings over the next hour. I cannot tell you the overwhelming sense of relief when my client was given a non-custodial sentence. It was a lesson I never forgot.

If the trial involves scrutiny of documents, always examine originals, not copies. Never be content with looking only at the face of them

Sir Rudolph Lyons, ultimately Recorder of Liverpool, and probably the most formidable cross-examiner I ever encountered at the Bar, taught me that he had often found manuscript notations on the back of documents that threw a great deal of light on their true significance that their face value did not reveal. This precept is still a valuable one, even though documents are increasingly displayed electronically and not in hard copy form.

When you are on your feet and examining or cross-examining a witness, always keep an eye on the judge and the jury

As far as you can, make sure that they are keeping up with your questions – and with the point that you are seeking to establish by those questions. If the jury have been issued with documents, be sure that all of them give the document under immediate scrutiny their careful attention. Set your pace to match that of the slowest individual who must fully understand the relevance of your questions. A constant awareness of what is going on around you is essential.

The danger of asking one question too many is something always to be borne in mind when conducting a cross-examination

Handling a witness who is hostile to your client's cause is rarely an easy task. If you have made some headway – exacted some concessions – do not be greedy. Too often, there is a temptation to push one's luck. The outcome may be a response from the witness that serves to undo all the good achieved by your earlier questions. One step forward, two steps back. Know when to sit down.

Sometimes, too, know when not to stand up

Be sufficiently astute to weigh up if a witness's evidence really demands public challenge, or whether, if you do start asking questions, you will not simply be offering unnecessary hostages to fortune. If a jury notes that you have not disputed a piece of evidence, they may instinctively not put weight on it, even though the other side may be relying on it.

Be courteous in your conduct and demeanour

There is rarely anything more destructive than the quiet demolition of a witness. A confrontational stance serves often to antagonize a witness and drive him or her into a more adamantly hostile attitude. How often have I seen dogmatic witnesses skilfully and gently led down a path into a position that insidiously serves to establish their unreliability – or worse –and from which they then, too late, desperately seek to escape. A wise judge once said that to cross-examine does not mean to examine crossly.

Never take advantage of your position to be gratuitously cruel or vindictive to a witness

This is not only dishonourable, but is almost invariably counter-productive in terms of its impact on a jury.

Do not forget that examination in chief of your own witness(es) is an art form, too

Try to identify and address the essential issues raised with simple questions that, wherever possible, admit of short answers. As far as you are able, remember that giving evidence in open court is for most people a unique and daunting experience. Do your best to put them at their ease.

Mention of extracting short answers brings back memories of a sleepy day at the Quarter Sessions of the West Riding of Yorkshire. I think I was sitting as deputy chairman. The accused was charged with the theft of a pig, and had elected for trial by jury. He had been found late one evening walking along a country road with the squealing piglet under his arm. His defence was that he had found it wandering in a lane, and was taking it to the local police station in an effort to trace the owner when he was apprehended. His arrest was all a terrible mistake. His counsel, Ian Boyd (the very same who in later life, as a magistrate in Hull, threw out the charge of conspiracy laid against my prison governor client), pointed out that the place he was caught was nowhere near the police station. 'Well,' said his client. 'I was lost.' Came this question: 'Please tell the jury exactly where you were when you discovered that you were lost?'

Beat that!

Courtesy and demeanour are best accompanied by deportment and by smart attire

It may seem old-fashioned, but a good posture and freshly crisp legal bands are a 'must'.

I have to acknowledge that, when all is said and done, you will still need luck

My life abundantly demonstrates that you need good luck in order to be in the right place at the right time; lucky in the cases that fall to your lot. Above all, perhaps, you need to be lucky enough to possess by sheer chance the native attributes to bring to bear on what for me was always the most competitive and individual of professions.

Everything you do as an advocate at the Bar should be founded on the bedrock of the interests of justice, and subordinate to that principle

Personal ambition drives most of us. It is an entirely laudable feature of life, but it must never obscure your chosen role as a servant of the machinery of justice. Henry Newbolt, the poet and philosopher, urged:

> To set the cause beyond renown,
> To love the game beyond the prize

As I re-read this primer to the aspiring young, I recognize that much of what I have to say could be met with the response that many of these precepts and cautions are at best subtle in their differences, and sometimes conflicting in their application. My only defence is to tell those who take up a career at the Bar that they will speedily come to discern the distinctions that I have sought to make, and to give effect to them in what I hope will be fulfilling and successful lives.

I remind myself of the man who was asked to describe a camel. His response was that he could not do so, but that he would certainly know one when he saw one.

5

A TRIBUTE
AND A TESTAMENT

I want now to say something about a most richly talented
advocate and friend who died some years ago. I shared
chambers with him in Leeds during nearly all my life at the
Bar. I worked or did forensic battle with him on countless
occasions, and I was privileged to give the tribute to him at
his memorial service in York Minster in 2011.

Gilbert Gray QC deserves mention not simply because he
was a kind and congenial man to so many (as he was), not
simply because he was my friend and cherished companion
(as he was), but because some of his oratory conveys at its
highest level what I mean by the art of the advocate. Before
I develop this statement, however, let me give you something
of the flavour of the man.

Gilbert Gray was a native of Scarborough, in North
Yorkshire. His father was a local butcher, part of a well-
known and active Methodist family. He was a practising
Christian all his life, only forsaking Methodism in his latter
years, when he was received into the Anglican Church. It
was his intention to himself to become a clergyman until
his time at Leeds University (where he became president of
the Students' Union). It was then and there that he decided
upon the Bar as his way of professional life. The loss to the
Church was the Bar's immeasurable gain. It was he who
persuaded me to leave my original chambers and to join

the thriving set of which he was a member, at 37 Park Square in Leeds.

Shortly after I did so (in, I think, 1963), he asked me to accompany him on an evening's trip from Leeds to Whitby, where he addressed three old ladies and a small dog in a disused chapel on behalf of the Liberal candidate for Scarborough and Whitby in that year's general election. When we set off on the return journey it was dark, and what is known in that part of the world as a 'sea fret' descended. The mist was so dense that you could only see about two cat's eyes on the road ahead. Gilbert was driving his latest motoring pride and joy, a Mark X Jaguar. As we headed west, and despite the silence within this grand barouche, I was increasingly conscious of a high speed quite incompatible with the prevailing visibility. I peered over at the speedometer, the needle of which hovered around 60 mph. The driver was impassive, clad in a Locke's bowler that served him both as a sartorial imperative and (I hazarded) perhaps a crash helmet. I ground my heels into the sheepskin carpet that adorned the interior. At last I was driven to speak. I pointed out that if by ill-chance there was a car parked on the nearside, then, in these conditions, I was in the death seat.

'I know, dear boy: that's why I'm driving on the wrong side of the road.'

Get the picture?

To his advocacy, then. Speaking in mitigation for a senior policeman who had descended so low as to lend himself to a part in a serious robbery, and who was heading for (and received) a double-figure prison sentence:

'My Lord, as he sits behind me in the dock, listening to these few words on his behalf, he looks out through a window of tears on to a world drenched in shame.'

Speaking in court on behalf of the Circuit Bar to voice

their tribute following the death of a very promising young barrister, and taking as his theme some words of A.E. Housman from *A Shropshire Lad*:

'As we bid him farewell, we know that he takes back, bright to the coiner, the mintage of man.'

Representing a man of otherwise good character who pleaded guilty to causing death by dangerous driving:

'No sentence that this court sees fit to impose upon my client can match his lifelong awareness that in a moment of fatal inadvertence by him, an innocent soul was swept into eternity.'

(I have a confession to make about this particular mitigation. The great man was not averse to using some of his more memorable pronouncements on more than one occasion. In one such instance I was prosecuting his client for the same offence. In mitigation, he reached the apotheosis of his remarks to the court, and began 'No sentence that this court sees fit to impose . . .' Of course, I knew what was coming, and in my seat next to him, in a loud stage whisper and with barely suppressed mirth, I said with a heavy sigh, 'Not *another* soul going to eternity?' Fortunately, my aside was taken in good part by the butt of my clumsy humour. I didn't deserve it.)

Nor were Gray's skills confined to the criminal scene. He represented a group of objectors before a planning inquiry in resisting an application by the then National Coal Board to operate open-cast mining in the Vale of Belvoir. Counsel for the Board, who over many days suffered a verbal drubbing at Gilbert's hands, spoke of him conducting himself 'like a Shakespearian actor-manager haranguing the groundlings'.

It is not surprising to know that he was one of the most accomplished after-dinner speakers in the country. The fees he commanded for these post-prandial performances were very large. I only learned after his death that he had given every penny of them to the RNLI. He was patron of the Scarborough lifeboat, and his ashes were scattered from it in the town's South Bay. (Shortly after the doctors gave him a terminal prognosis, he was visited by the coxswain of the lifeboat. He said to the great man that he understood that his wish was that his remains should be cremated. In those circumstances, the lifeboat crew at Scarborough would count it a privilege if the ashes were to be scattered from that vessel into the sea off the town. Gilbert's reply was typical of the man. 'I am greatly touched and flattered. I would like that very much,' he said, 'but please choose a calm day, because I am prone to sea-sickness!')

I can remember doing battle with him in a case at York. In the middle of the trial, a helicopter bore him at the end of the day to the Isle of Wight, where he spoke before a distinguished company and was flown back the next morning to resume his part in the trial. On another occasion, HRH The Duke of Edinburgh was guest of honour at the annual dinner of the Professional Footballers Association in London. GG responded on behalf of the guests. It was a time when professional football presented an ugly face. All but the richest few clubs played at grounds whose facilities were primitive and (as the Hillsborough disaster would demonstrate) wholly unfit for purpose. Crowd violence was commonplace. Gilbert said of this to HRH, 'As ever, a senior member of the royal family is among the first to be present at the scene of a national disaster.'

More was to come. To make sense of what follows, you must understand that at the time there existed a particular form of sentence which was effectively one of life imprisonment, but which for technical reasons was defined in archaic language as 'Detention during Her Majesty's Pleasure'. In the course of his speech GG turned to HRH and said, 'Every criminal lawyer, Your Royal Highness, is familiar with the term, "Her Majesty's Pleasure" – but very few of us are privileged to meet him.' The Duke was convulsed with laughter.

It is no wonder that a distinguished fellow Silk said of GG that he made him feel as though English was his second language. Had GG been a Silk in Edwardian days, his every word would have been proclaimed on the front pages. As it is, I count myself thrice fortunate to have been a colleague in the days when he adorned our profession and our lives.

Two other aspects of his life always remain with me. First, he never went to the bench. Perhaps the legal establishment considered him too idiosyncratic to fit the office. Perhaps he never wished for it. I don't know; I never asked him. Second (as I have already said), behind the flippant entertainer lay a person whose understated Christian beliefs were profound. At the funeral of a much-loved mutual friend he reminded us that the deceased's creed was to be found thus: 'Fear knocked on the door. Faith opened it. There was no one there.' Precisely the same could be said of the man who spoke those words on that day. His abiding faith was the rock around which swirled the ceaseless currents of his long and splendid life.

Lest it be thought that I have over-egged this particular pudding, let me say that Gilly Gray was, by common consent, not only the most popular common-law Silk of his generation, but the best-loved. He was an ornament to my profession. To the lives of many, not least myself, he was a shining beacon.

Before I bid a final farewell to my retrospect of life at the Bar, I need to say something more about the huge role played in it by the barrister's clerk. I have already expressed my deep thanks to my very first clerk, Frank Davies. It was he who afforded me my first chances to prove my worth. He it was, certainly, who kick-started my progress. But his assistance and influence did not end there. By no means.

On a daily basis, the clerk's impact on the fees a barrister earned was a constant. First, in all paid (as opposed to legal aid) work, it was the clerk's responsibility to negotiate a fee with the solicitor wishing to instruct you. In those days, the rule widely applied by sets of chambers was that the clerk's total remuneration was based upon 10 per cent of the fees earned (including legal aid) by each and every member of his 'stable'. There was, therefore, a powerful personal incentive for him to secure as high a fee as possible for all the work coming into chambers. It might be paper work, such as a request for counsel's opinion on the merits of a proposed civil claim for damages, or the brief for the conduct of a case – civil or criminal – in court. Negotiating skills were obviously a prime asset. No decent clerk ever undervalued the services of a member of his chambers.

When I moved from Vince's Chambers to 37 Park Square in Leeds, my new clerk was the late Ernest Shackleton. As a fee negotiator, he was a nonpareil. A brief incursion into vulgarity is essential to illustrate his talent. It also serves to illustrate the supreme confidence of a clerk who had an astute awareness of the prevailing market value of 'his' men.

Ernest was nothing if not robust. One morning, I walked into his office in chambers. He was on the phone. It was plain that the solicitor at the other end of the line had just proposed a fee. Ernest was incredulous. 'Fifty guineas!' he exploded. 'Fifty guineas – I wouldn't allow my Mr Gray even to fart for fifty guineas!' I don't know the ultimate outcome of those negotiations, but I bet that the solicitor was not for a moment deterred from his choice of counsel, and that when the brief was delivered the agreed fee fully reflected Ernest's professed outrage.

The commission basis for a clerk's income has now long gone, but it had a corollary worth noting. You may easily imagine that if the clerk was serving a strong set of chambers, his income usually exceeded that of all but the most successful and sought-after of its members. In my latter days at the Bar I had chambers both in Leeds and in the Temple in London. My London chambers numbered, probably, some eight or ten busy Silks, and twice as many juniors. Ten per cent of their aggregate income was, to my mind, riches beyond the dreams of avarice. I recall one early summer day when my London clerk said to me (without the slightest trace of embarrassment) that should my family ever need a break in the sun he would be very happy to let me have the use of his villa in Spain.

Apart from what I will describe as 'brokerage' skills, there was another area in which the clerk could be of considerable assistance in maximizing fee income. This was particularly so in the days before Crown Courts replaced the old system of Quarter Sessions and Assizes.

The timetable of the visiting High Court Judges sitting at assize in major cities was crammed into a very short period. Usually, it was but a few weeks when two or three judges would visit. So there was great pressure on the courts' administration to ensure that all those judges were kept as fully occupied as possible with work of High Court calibre.

If you were a busy Silk, there was a serious risk that this system would create a clash between your various commitments, because two of your briefs might be listed on the same day before two different judges. If that could not be avoided, then you had to return one of your briefs to other counsel. And if that happened, you lost the fee marked on the brief, and (unless it was returned to another member of your chambers) your clerk lost his 10 per cent.

The decision as to which cases should be listed before which judge at any given time rested with the courts listing officer. You can appreciate that the clerks from all the affected chambers jockeyed with each other in a sustained effort to ensure that their men were not confronted with a clash of that kind. If their man was to appear before Mr Justice A in Court 1, then it was vital that no other of his cases should be listed at the same time before Mr Justice B in Court 2. Shortly put, to be kept out of the list was very good news.

I have already spoken of Ernest Shackleton. He had been an outstanding clerk to me. Among other qualities, he always struck the right balance between being too deferential to me, and being too matey. So he middled it by always addressing me by my initials, HHO. There came a time when, sadly, he became terminally ill.

On this most melancholy of occasions I sat by his bedside. 'Well, HHO,' he said, 'you know that I have always tried to be a good clerk to you in every way' (pause) 'and when the Day of Judgement comes, I promise that I will do my best for you to keep you out of the list.'

Bless his memory.

Before I am finally done with clerks, I must speak of a clerk of a different order. On appointment, all High Court Judges are assigned a personal clerk who serves them both in London and on circuit. In my time, these men were often from a police or military background. Their role is so all-encompassing and invaluable that it is difficult to define. They are a kind of PA. They have clerical duties; they deal with your official correspondence; they keep your diary of engagements. They are your liaison between the courts where you sit and, when on circuit, the lodgings that are provided throughout the kingdom for judges as their temporary home. They sit with you on the bench. They stay in the lodgings with you. They act as a kind of valet. They are called upon to perform countless little tasks which make them a sort of general factotum. You will readily understand that they become indispensable.

It was my very great good luck that from the pool of available candidates I chose Bob John – a recently retired Metropolitan Police inspector – to be my clerk. His unswerving loyalty, his common sense, his kindness and his constant cheerfulness were beyond measure. He became a confidant, a companion, and a most trusted support. My gratitude to him is boundless.

6

SCARLET AND ERMINE

I became the Hon. Mr Justice Ognall on 13 January 1986, and shortly afterwards – with a ceremony at Buckingham Palace – became a member of the Society of Knights Bachelor. (On an entirely familial note, I recall telling my dear mother-in-law Florence Scott that my appointment carried with it a knighthood. 'There you are, Granny,' I said, 'Sally is now a Lady.' Reply: 'My daughter has always been a lady.' Properly rebuked!)

I had always regarded appointment to the High Court as the most desirable recognition of standing in my profession. I have already hinted that it was also very welcome to me by this stage of my career. I had grown ever wearier of the exacting demands that Silk made upon me. Building and achieving a reputation is one thing. Experience shows that maintaining it to the standards now expected of you is quite another.

My own appointment, and the system of appointments as a whole, are worth a mention. When I was invited by the Lord Chancellor, Lord Hailsham, to join the High Court bench, you may be surprised to know that had I been asked how I (or anybody else) was identified as suitable, I would have been hard-pressed to offer a knowledgeable answer. Essentially, I believe that soundings were taken among the existing senior judiciary as to their assessment of the (generally) QCs who appeared before them, and the 'short list' would be reviewed by the Lord Chief Justice, the Master of the Rolls (the head of the civil justice division) and the senior judge of both the Chancery and Family divisions.

That's how it generally worked. But luck had a role to play sometimes, and certainly in my case I know how it happened – and perceived ability had nothing to do with it. Three months before I received the nod, I was one of those attending an annual seminar run by the Judicial Studies Board for keeping Recorders and newly appointed permanent judges up to speed.

We were visited for a pep talk by the then Deputy Chief Justice, Lord Justice Watkins, VC. At a question and answer session there was a discussion as to the principles on which remission of sentence and parole licence for life-sentence prisoners were applied. I stood up and suggested that the early release of long-sentence inmates was an essentially covert practice; few of the public were aware that when a judge passed, for example, a sentence of fifteen years it could be – and often was – the case that the sentence served was actually much less. In my opinion, I said, this would be seen by many as hypocritical lip service, directed to assuaging public concern about serious crime while in fact not doing anything of the kind. I brazenly suggested that the system meant that the judiciary were thus being required to lend themselves to a highly publicized con trick.

It so happened that (wholly unbeknown to me) this was a hobby horse that Tasker Watkins had been riding for some time. And I am quite certain that my comments were not only taken on board, but also relayed elsewhere.

The seminar took place in September 1985. Is it any coincidence that in early December I was summoned to see the Lord Chancellor? And within three months of my appointment I became chairman of the Criminal Committee of the Judicial Studies Board. That afforded me a bird's eye view for the next three years of others following in my footsteps in impertinently killing sacred cows of the justice system! So, my appointment is surely a classic example of being in the right place at the right time, and I don't hesitate to admit it.

Today, the appointment system is totally different. The procedure is clearly defined, and application (yes, it's no longer good manners to wait until asked) and interview are part of it. But I do not see any real difference in calibre between those appointed in my time and those appointed now. I firmly believe that the public can continue to repose every confidence in the higher judiciary. Reliable informants do tell me, however, that the highest ranks have fallen into an insidious trap laid by the executive in elevating case-management and targets into a necessary part of the judicial armoury.

A good example is what are known as 'cracked trials', that is, cases listed as trials to occupy an estimated period of time, but which on the appointed day turn into guilty pleas. You might have thought this would be welcome news. Indeed, there has long been a hallowed principle of our criminal law that a plea of guilty, as a token of remorse, generally attracts a lesser sentence. But I am told that the disturbance to the timetable caused by these cases is for that very reason viewed in some quarters of the administration as disrupting the orderly progress of the list, despite the vital fact that the change of plea reflects the just disposal of the case.

This has a resonance within our NHS, where a top-heavy bureaucracy is said to be overwhelming effective medical practice. Is that comparison a coincidence?

———

And so to life on the bench. It started, hilariously, in this way.

Lord Lane was my first boss as Lord Chief Justice. He

was a delightful man, and was deservedly held in universal respect by the profession. He had enjoyed a splendid record during the Second World War as a pilot with transport command. He had been a formidable advocate on the Midland & Oxford Circuit while at the Bar. As a judge, he was a classic promoter of the common-sense approach to problems. That is not to decry his intellectual qualities, but he did not hesitate to say to himself, 'If that's said to be the law, it's an ass', and to pronounce accordingly.

Like all new judges, I was summoned to meet him. It was a most congenial occasion. When it was over, he had plainly got the measure of me. He afterwards sent me a copy of the local Nottingham newspaper, reporting a scandalous event that had transfixed the population of the city (and, no doubt, a wider audience) in the late nineteenth century.

It involved a High Court Judge sitting at the Nottingham Assizes, and therefore staying in the local judges' lodgings. On this particular morning, the butler came to his Lordship's bedroom with his morning tea and newspaper. To his surprise, the bedroom was unoccupied, and the bed had plainly not been slept in the previous night. The judge was nowhere to be seen. There was a hue and cry.

The police were alerted. It did not take very long before the missing judge was found. The body lay in a brothel near High Pavement, in the centre of the city.

Discretion was imperative. The corpse was smuggled back via the servants' entrance to the lodgings, and into his Lordship's bed. Word was put about that Mr Justice X had died peacefully in his sleep.

Since this was a sudden, unexplained death, an inquest was necessary. This is where the attempted cover-up came unstuck. Unfortunately, the coroner for the city had himself but recently died. History might otherwise have told a different tale. As it was, the assistant coroner was a zealous young fellow, who had concerns and instigated a thorough investigation. The scandalous truth finally emerged.

At the inquest, the prostitute who had been the deceased's last companion on this earth was called to give evidence. The nub of her testimony was to be found in the next day's edition of the newspaper, the extract from which Lord Lane copied to me: 'And then,' she said, 'the old gentleman groaned, and rolled away, and I thought he had come – but he'd gone.'

I promise you, it is true. I still have the newspaper cutting.

The verbatim report was accompanied by a manuscript note to me saying 'Harry, let this be a warning to you.' Our meeting had ended with Lord Lane telling me that if I ever encountered problems while out on circuit, I must feel free to get in touch. In the light of his subsequent missive, I have often wondered what problems he had in mind.

It had been at Lord Lane's invitation that I became, very shortly after my appointment to the bench, chairman of the Criminal Committee of the Judicial Studies Board. In that capacity, I had three most interesting and enjoyable years in charge of seminars designed to train new Recorders, as well as High Court Judges whose specialized practices had not involved criminal cases, in the judicial conduct of criminal trials. I also had a three-year spell as vice-chairman of the Parole Board and chairman of its Life Sentence Review Committee. Additionally (like most judges of the High Court), I sat with two others hearing criminal appeals in the Court of Appeal in London. My time on the Parole Board was a challenging one, and I think deserves mention.

If and when, and under what constraints, a prisoner serving

a life sentence is deemed fit for release inevitably imposes a special burden on those who make the decision. Quite often, even when a prisoner has served a very substantial period 'inside', and there is a complete consensus from the prison and medical staff supporting the application, it is still refused. There may be a number of reasons for this. Of course, the overriding consideration must be the risk to the public. Putting that to one side, there are other relevant consider-ations. One such situation arises when, in the view of the reviewing committee, the gravity of the crime for which the sentence was passed is such that it has to be marked by a period of detention that is much longer than normal – not excluding what is now called 'whole life'. Presently, the responsibility for making such decisions lies with the High Court, by means of a further review. But I have no doubt that even when a whole-life term has not been ordered, and the applicant has crossed the time threshold for their first application, the board may still form their own assessment of the gravity of the crime and, taking account of that, reject the application.

In my day, we had before us an application by Myra Hindley, one of the two so-called Moors Murderers. The nature of their crimes was clearly such that there would have been an unanswerable public outcry at any decision that she should be released on parole.

I recall that case not simply for its unparalleled wickedness, but also for the fact that for many years Myra Hindley was the subject of a sustained campaign, led by a hereditary peer, to secure her parole. It was maintained that she had under-gone a complete change of character, and was now a devout Christian who had 'seen the light'. I had something to say about this when we reviewed the application. What, I asked, of the parents of the five kids who, with Brady, she had tortured, violated, murdered and buried on a bleak Pennine moorland? For them, an impenetrable and terrible darkness had descended in which they were to be enshrouded for the rest of their tortured lives. Even allowing for the true and unshakeable convictions of the devout Christian, there have to be times when the divine quality of forgiveness lies permanently forfeit.

Hindley was to die in prison in 2002, after thirty-six years' detention. Her partner in the commission of those most evil and depraved of crimes, Ian Brady, died in 2017. He had then been detained for over fifty years.

I do bear in mind that in the case of fixed-term (as opposed to life) sentences, there are times when the impact of parole on the actual time served is something of which the public at large is unaware. I became in that sense the unwitting ally of Lord Justice Watkins in speaking out as I did. That said, it should be remembered that when a court passing a life sentence sets out the earliest date on which an application for parole on life licence may be made, it should not be confused with a belief that release on that occasion will necessarily follow. How often do I hear people say 'Oh, he'll be out after x years'? I hope I have said enough to show that if you hold to that view, you are seriously mistaken.

Putting aside those sort of duties, the great proportion of my life as a judge was spent, either in London or in cities throughout England and Wales, presiding over trials involving the most serious criminal offences.

There were civil actions too. One of my very first cases as a judge was a class action against the Department of Health, brought on behalf of hundreds of haemophiliacs who had contracted HIV through contaminated blood transfusions.

There were formidable legal difficulties in the way of the claims. Mindful of this, I wrote in confidence to the Secretary of State for Health, pointing out the problem to him and inviting government in all the circumstances to consider a compassionate approach to the issue of compensation. I am happy to say that it seemed to prove of some help to the claimants. Their cases were settled.

(At the time of writing, and over thirty years after the matter came before me, the Prime Minister announced the setting up of an inquiry into the issues raised, and what she describes as the 'appalling injustice' suffered by those who were infected. All that I can say is that I am reminded of the aphorism that 'Justice delayed is justice denied'. The law as it stood denied them full compensation. Will there now be full redress, by what route, and what of those (no doubt many) who have since died?)

In the fourteen years that I sat in the Queen's Bench Division, the agenda offered by the lists was extensive. I shall try to offer my recollections of just a few cases that I hope will illustrate the nature of the job and which, by virtue of their circumstances, stand out in my mind. All but one of these were cases in which I was sitting outside London, on circuit. Before I leave London on these traveller's recollections, however, let me describe to you sitting in London, either at the Royal Courts of Justice on the Strand, or at the Central Criminal Court, eastwards down the road.

I sat at the Central Criminal Court (the Old Bailey) a few times, but it was essentially the domain of the City of London, and its ceremonials did not fit in well with my temperament. I recall, for example, the fact that any High Court Judge assigned to sit there along with the permanent Old Bailey judges was bidden each day to a grand lunch with the Sheriffs of the City of London and distinguished guests from all walks of life. You may imagine that the prospect of a three-course meal (with appropriate liquid refreshment, if you wished it) was not, for me, conducive to the judicial job in hand, and when I tell you that it was expected that one would remain fully robed during the meal, you will no doubt get my drift. I acknowledge the intended hospitality, but there is a time and a place . . .

Turning to the Royal Courts, and in telling you this tale I move from what some might characterize as the sublime, to the ridiculous. The Law Courts (as they are known) are housed in a truly enormous building. Victorian Gothic, opened by Queen Victoria in 1882, it contains literally miles of corridors. Most High Court Judges have a permanent room in the building. Access to any of the countless court-rooms often entails a very long walk. I have known my clerk undertake a preliminary reconnaissance in order to determine where I was bound. So it was that on one occasion I was to sit in a distant room that was wholly unfamiliar to me.

It was a civil action. Having entered from the red-carpeted corridor and bowed to counsel, I was asked to retire again for a short time because the parties were on the brink of settling the action. I stood up, bowed, turned round, opened what I thought was the door through which I had made my initial entrance, and walked through it. There was an almighty crash as I collided at once with a bucket containing a broom. I had walked into the cleaners' cupboard.

I paused; behind me, I could hear the unrepressed sounds of mirth. Doing my best to preserve an outward appearance of dignity, I backed out, turned round and – with a pale smile – this time found the right exit.

For the purposes of this memoir, enough of sitting in London. And so to the serious business of some of my cases sitting on circuit.

KEITH JOHN ROSE

Ransom

On a fine autumn morning in 1981, forty-two-year-old Juliet Rowe was at home in the house in Budleigh Salterton, Devon, that she shared with her husband. He was the wealthy owner of a supermarket business.

She was alone. Photographs subsequently taken show that she was doing some domestic chores. At the foot of the stairs was a neat pile of freshly ironed clothing.

Wholly unknown to her, her life was within moments of its peremptory end, and in the most brutal way. Into the house there came abruptly a man armed with a loaded Colt pistol. He was intent on taking her captive for ransom. Juliet Rowe would not submit, and in terror sought to flee from him. He pursued her around the house. It was obviously clear to him that – at whatever price – she must not be able to identify him later. As she was fleeing from him, he shot her no less than four times in the back. When finally she fell, he stood over her and shot her twice more, through the head and the heart.

The identity of the murderer remained unsolved for nearly ten years, until the kidnapping for ransom (again in Devon) of a wealthy young businessman. The intruder bound and gagged his victim's parents, and then took his hostage. He was taken to a woodland, where he was himself bound and gagged, handcuffed to a tree and left with a wire noose around his neck. There was a ransom demand for £1 million. Remarkably, the victim was discovered after four days, still alive.

Investigation revealed that the perpetrator was a man named Keith John Rose. For those offences, he was sentenced to fifteen years' imprisonment. In the course of extensive

enquiries into his crimes, evidence emerged that clearly impli-
cated him in the killing of Mrs Rowe so many years before.
It happened in this way. Because it had been another case
involving ransom, the police saw Mr Rowe again. It turned
out that, four weeks before committing the later crimes,
Keith Rose had spoken to Mr Rowe in a public house and
effectively boasted that he had been interviewed by the police
after the murder of Mrs Rowe. Presciently, that led the
police to reopen their ten-year-old enquiries – and this time
with a successful outcome. Hence his appearance before me
at Exeter Crown Court. The jury convicted him of her
murder, and I sentenced him to life imprisonment. (If you
recall my account of Thomas Anderson's return to Veleta
Cottage in Leeds after he had killed Daisy Morris there, I
wonder again why it is that in so many instances, sooner or
later, the murderer feels compelled voluntarily to connect
himself with his crime?)

Four year later, in 1995, Rose escaped from Parkhurst
high security prison. In his cell was found a 'hit list' of people
upon whom he was apparently set on exacting revenge. My
name was among them. Rose was recaptured after some five
days, and remains in prison. What I remember of those
events is that while he was at large it seems that a senior
police officer went on TV and said that all those listed had
been alerted. I say 'it seems' because I did not see the
broadcast. I was on holiday in France at the time. Neither
then nor later, however, was I alerted by the police to these
events. I only came upon the information by chance when
I saw a subsequent news item. I suppose that it is inherently
in the nature of the work of any judge involved in a criminal
trial that they may be vulnerable in this way.

On only one other occasion in my life was I the subject
of a threat, and that was when I was sitting as a Recorder
in Yorkshire. The phone call I received did not suggest any

truly serious intention in the mind of the caller, and that proved to be the case. Like all other judges it was necessary for me to have confidence in the system designed to safeguard us, even if – as my French leave showed – there was sometimes a breakdown in communication.

You may believe you see why the case had at least one memorable feature for me, in the prospect (however remote) that my work had placed me or my family in a position of personal danger. If you think that, you would be wrong. Its true and much greater significance in my story is that I often still think of Juliet Rowe's last terrifying moments, and of the two final, purposeful shots that brought them to an end, as she lay grievously wounded at her assailant's feet.

———•———

Euthanasia is, understandably, a vexed and controversial subject on which many people on either side hold strong and entrenched views. My encounter at the sharp end of this issue came at Winchester Crown Court in September 1992.

(I loved sitting at Winchester. Given the chance, I opted to go there as a judge on a number of occasions. The city is by common consent a favourite place among the judges who travel Circuits. The lodgings have a lovely setting in the Cathedral Close and Hampshire is a beautiful county. I shall not forget my first encounter at Winchester railway station with the chauffeur of the car that came to meet me. As with many cities, the authorities hired the limousine from a local firm who also carry on business as undertakers – hence the large black Daimler. The driver in this instance, Eric, engaged me in conversation on the journey. I suggested to him that it must be a refreshing change to drive her Majesty's judges instead of forming part of a funeral cortege.

'Not really,' he said. 'After all, most of you judges are nearly dead.')

DR NIGEL COX

Mercy

A consultant rheumatologist at the Royal Hampshire County Hospital, Dr Cox was tried upon an allegation that in August 1991, he had attempted to murder an elderly patient, Lillian Boyes. The trial raised in the starkest form the issue of euthanasia and the law's response to it. My inclusion of the circumstances of this most unhappy and testing case is justified, I believe, if only because to my knowledge Dr Cox remains the only medical practitioner to be convicted in this country for involvement of whatever nature in a mercy killing.

Mrs Boyes was seventy years old, and a patient of Dr Cox for some thirteen years. By the time she was admitted to the hospital on this occasion, she was in constant agony. It was clear that her life was within hours of its end, and by natural causes. Despite that, she and her family implored Dr Cox to hasten its conclusion. He did so, injecting her with twice the fatal dose of potassium chloride. She died within minutes.

For all any of us may know, this sort of thing may take place on numerous occasions. If the relatives involved are like the family of Mrs Boyes, they understandably and avidly welcome it. Certainly, they say nothing public about it. In this instance, however, Dr Cox entered his administration of the fatal dosage into the hospital log. Why he chose to do so remains a mystery. Even with the medication on record, the death would probably have gone unremarked save that a senior nurse of strong religious convictions noticed the log entry and reported it to her superiors. And so the wheels were set in motion which led Dr Cox to Winchester Crown Court.

You may ask why, if Dr Cox was to be tried at all, he was not charged with murder rather than attempted murder? The answer lay in the fact that the body of Mrs Boyes had been speedily cremated; there had been no autopsy. Therefore, the possibility, however remote, that she had succumbed to natural causes *before* the fatal injection could take effect could not be wholly excluded. In those circumstances, the prosecution's case was that whatever the actual cause of death, there could be no doubt of Dr Cox's intention in doing what he had done. It was in this way that the allegation was framed as one of attempted murder.

The jury convicted the doctor, and I was faced with the extremely difficult task of deciding on the appropriate sentence. He eventually received a suspended sentence of twelve months' imprisonment. A few weeks later, in November 1992, the Professional Conduct Committee of the General Medical Council decided that in the circumstances it was unnecessary for them to take any further disciplinary action. In February 1993, Dr Cox resumed his position as a consultant, although under supervision.

Some time later, when I was the speaker at a medico-legal gathering in London, Dr Cox was among the audience and sought to question me about the trial. It was a highly embarrassing moment.

PETER KITE

A warning ignored

This case deserves inclusion for a number of reasons, including the fact that it was the first time that a company – as opposed to an individual – had been charged with and convicted of unlawful killing (manslaughter). But there was in my experience one feature of the evidence that made the case remarkable. That feature will emerge.

Peter Kite owned a company – Active Learning & Leisure – offering adventure activities for youngsters. One of those activities was canoeing on inshore waters. The evidence established that this 'adventure', as organized by the company, was a serious accident waiting to happen. A terrifying catalogue of inadequate training of the participants, inexperienced and incompetent supervision and lack of proper safety equipment proved to be a recipe for a fatal disaster.

On 22 March 1993 the company organized a canoe trip across Lyme Bay for a group of teenagers from a Plymouth community college. Almost as soon as the party paddled away from shore, the canoes were swept inexorably out to sea. The supervisors were unable to address the situation, and gave the wrong advice to the group. Communication with the shore was ineffective. Several canoes overturned, and by the time lifeboat and helicopter assistance arrived four of the group had drowned. Only good fortune prevented more deaths.

The investigation that followed led to the prosecution for manslaughter of Peter Kite, his company and the manager of the company's adventure centre (who was ultimately acquitted). The case for the prosecution rested on a well-recognized principle, namely that to cause the death of another by conduct so negligent as to be considered reckless amounts to the offence of unlawful killing. The company, as opposed to any individual, would likewise be guilty if the jury concluded that the central controllers of the company – its guiding hands – had acted in such a way. Thus it was alleged that the defendants, well knowing that the venture at Lyme Bay carried with it obvious risks of fatality, nonetheless went on with the activity and that those risks in fact materialized. In doing so, the case was that their conduct was so heedless of the potential consequences as to demand the conclusion that they had been reckless, and had so caused the deaths. Kite and his company were convicted on that basis.

The striking feature of the evidence given at the trial that has stuck in my mind since then was that given by two young instructors who were former employees of Active Learning & Leisure. Appalled by the nature and extent of the safety deficiencies in the set-up, they resigned some nine months before the catastrophe, and wrote to Peter Kite in the following terms: 'We think that you should take a careful look at your standards of safety, or you may find yourself trying to explain why someone's son or daughter is not coming home.'

In my long experience, there surely could never have been a more explicit warning of the destination to which the ventures were heading, unless the whole organization was put right. It is that aspect of the case that makes it so noteworthy even now.

The company was fined. Peter Kite was sentenced by me to three years' imprisonment, reduced to two years on appeal. This case was the direct impetus for legislation in 1995 that established a system of statutory control of adventure activities.

I come now to the last of my judicial retrospectives. Although the last, it is most assuredly not the least. An account of it discloses a tale so curious and memorable as to justify the epithet 'unique'.

COLIN STAGG

Vindication

On the warm and sunny morning of 15 July 1992 an attractive twenty-three-year-old woman, Rachel Nickell, accompanied
by her two-year-old son Alex, was walking her dog on
Wimbledon Common. She was sexually assaulted, stabbed
several times, and her throat was cut. Her little son was
discovered clinging to her bloodstained body, saying 'Wake
up, Mummy.'

The murder and the ensuing investigation attracted
immense publicity. The Metropolitan Police were under the
most intense pressure to make an arrest. Their enquiries led
them nowhere. (The ultimate cost of the investigation was
later put at £3 million.) In what can only be described as a
state of increasing desperation, police attention fell upon a
man who lived in the district and was known to walk his
dog on the common.

His name was Colin Stagg. A single man, living alone, he
was viewed by some of his neighbours as weird and unattractive. He was interested in the occult. He had no
convictions of any kind, but everything about him made him
a soft target for the police.

They sought advice from a criminal psychologist, Paul
Britton, and obtained from him a criminal profile of the
killer. They decided that Stagg fitted the profile. With the
assistance of Mr Britton, they set out to entice Stagg into
making admissions to the crime, via a process I later described
as 'a honey trap'.

A policewoman using the name 'Lizzie James' was used
to spring the trap. Equipped with a voice recorder, she was
deputed to contact Stagg and to engage him in telephone
conversations as frequently as possible. She did just that, and

the several hours of conversation thus obtained were transcribed. On the basis of that material alone, the police and the Crown Prosecution Service concluded that they revealed a case against Stagg upon which a jury could properly and safely be invited to convict him of the murder of Rachel Nickell. They arrested him for it. Their confidence was woefully misplaced.

Colin Stagg was tried by me and a jury at the Old Bailey in September 1994. It was common ground that the case for the prosecution stood or failed entirely on their submission that the dialogues with 'Lizzie James' contained comments by Stagg from which it could safely and surely be inferred that he was admitting the murder of Rachel Nickell. For that reason, counsel agreed before me that the introduction of the remainder of the essentially uncontroversial evidence should be deferred until after the 'honey trap' transcripts had been addressed. In accordance with practice, William Clegg QC for the defence said that he wanted that material to be introduced initially in the absence of the jury. His challenge to it, he said, would lie principally in the contention that – irrespective of any proven weight that might be given to it – the evidence had been obtained unlawfully. If that was the case, then it would not be admissible for the jury's consideration. The second limb of his argument would be that, in any event, even if the evidence were to be ruled admissible, a careful appraisal of it would reveal nothing at all of an incriminating character. On either footing, the prosecution would have no probative material. In that event, their case was doomed.

The transcripts were introduced into evidence. I then heard counsel's submissions about their admissibility and the proper interpretation of their true effect from both sides. After that stage, I was entirely satisfied of two things. First, that the conduct of the police revealed to my mind (as I later expressed it) 'deception of the grossest kind'. I had no doubt that it was a very clear example of infringement of the rules forbidding attempts to secure confession from a person who had not been cautioned. My second conclusion has rarely been highlighted in reports, but was of crucial importance to the outcome of my ruling. What I hope was a scrupulously careful analysis of all the material (assisted by both leading counsel) disclosed to my mind nothing capable of supporting the case against the accused. (He made one remark that could be said to suggest he knew something that could only have been known by the murderer. But, at best, it was equivocal in nature, and in any event, it might have been the subject of prior general publicity.)

Overall, then, I was confronted by the clearest breaches of the rules governing the interrogation of suspects, as well as the fact that the evidence obtained in that fashion did nothing to advance the prosecution case.

Even had I taken a contrary view of the entrapment and of Stagg's single equivocal remark, and allowed it to go before the jury, the tidal wave of revulsion and hatred attached to the case carried with it, in my judgement, a serious risk that the jury might attach weight to it that it could not and should not properly bear. On whatever approach, I therefore ruled that the transcripts were not to be admitted before the jury. I have already made it plain that, bereft of that material, the prosecution were left with nothing. They dropped the case. I directed the jury to acquit, and they did so.

Two consequences followed. First, I immediately became the subject of sustained vilification by the media, often couched in hysterical terms. On the day following the conclusion of the trial, one national tabloid had as its front-page banner headline 'Judge in the dock'. This was based on the expressed reaction of representatives (of fairly humble rank in both instances) of the Crown Prosecution Service and the police. The same newspaper conducted over a period of many years a sustained campaign against my ruling that can only be described as a vendetta. Several papers openly suggested that by deciding as I did, I had lent myself to a perversion of the course of justice. The recurring theme was that I, as trial judge, had literally allowed Colin Stagg to get away with murder. However broad judicial shoulders must necessarily be, it was painful stuff for me and for my family.

The second outcome of the trial's conclusion will tell you why I – and many others – found it to be unique. Fourteen years after Stagg had walked free, that is to say in 2006, a so-called cold case review team went to Broadmoor Hospital in Berkshire. Their purpose was to interview a man named Robert Napper. They were armed with the results of much more sophisticated DNA analyses. Napper had been detained indefinitely in that high security institution following his conviction for the murders in 1993 of a woman and her four-year-old daughter – sixteen months after the murder on Wimbledon Common. Robert Napper admitted that it was he who had killed Rachel Nickell. In December 2008, at the same court where Colin Stagg had been acquitted following my ruling, Napper pleaded guilty to that terrible crime.

The policewoman who had played the role of Lizzie James quit the force and received £100,000 from it for the stress that she had endured playing the part. Colin Stagg received £700,000 for his wrongful arrest and prosecution. Young Alex, who had been with his mother when she was killed, was paid some £20,000 for her death. Many people thought that the disparity in amounts was bizarre.

What, as they say, was in it for me? Of course, no monetary compensation could be forthcoming. It was my job – unless I chose, possibly, to sue for defamation. That would have been a singularly unlikely scenario. For my part, I still await a public and equally prominent apology from the press who put me in the dock. Long experience has, however, taught me not to hold my breath. I know that there will never be an apology from anyone. A free press is an imperative, but those who trumpet its cause so stridently far too often forget that such freedom carries with it commensurate responsibilities. Unfortunately, it is my experience that a combination of arrogance and the insatiable demands for circulation together brook no denial.

I have spoken elsewhere of courage being a necessary part of the advocate's armoury. Sometimes courage is also needed by a trial judge. I hope that I am not being unduly cynical when I say that what was characterized by the media as my gross irresponsibility at the time that I discharged Stagg from custody at the end of his trial became, after Robert Napper's admission in 2006, a basis for recognizing and applauding judicial courage.

The arrogance of the media, and the judicial quality needed to confront it, received their synthesis when addressed in formidable terms by Boris Johnson in an article in the *Daily Telegraph* in June 2006:

> Today I salute the genius of a judge. If I had anything to do with the honours system I would be advising that the next list should contain a special medal for Mr Justice Ognall, and that the citation should recognize his conspicuous gallantry under fire. The Stagg case is a perfect example of why we should not allow ourselves to be ruled by tabloid editors . . . it needs brave politicians to resist this kind of nonsense, and brave judges to tell the media when they are wrong.

I hope that I will be forgiven the reproduction of this commentary. It is not prompted by any spirit of self-aggrandizement. It is there because it addresses an issue that I suggest is of fundamental importance to the continued well-being of society. The concept of free speech is increasingly invoked to defend the indefensible. It is in danger of becoming a shibboleth when it is pitted against the principle of an independent judiciary manifestly doing no more than its bounden duty. I recall with a sense of total repugnance the occasion in 2017 when three judges sitting as a Divisional Court of the High Court, and presided over by Lord Thomas, the Lord Chief Justice, ruled that as a matter of law, the royal prerogative could not be used to set in train our exit from the European Union; only Parliament had that power. (A decision, incidentally, upheld with a decisive majority by the full complement of judges of the Supreme Court.) A non-tabloid daily newspaper that is supposed to pride itself on its standards published on its front page a photograph of the three judges, with the headline 'Enemies of the people'. It is my contention that such disgraceful rabble-rousing reveals the true identity of those who are the people's enemy.

Speaking of arrogance, it is very rare indeed that a judge can – or should – say publicly 'I got it right', and have cast-iron assurance of it. In the case of R v Colin Stagg I shall always have the comfort of that awareness, and that is as good a time as any for me to cease these tales from the bench.

———

It is also a time for me to say how I look back on my time in scarlet and ermine, after the heady days of Silk. Well, let's start with some fun, though it is at a premium in my experience. Much of it is at the expense of the judges, who are still often thought of as stuffy and out of touch. I think that this is generally unfair today, but I do rejoice in a no doubt apocryphal tale that was circulating in the Law Courts in the Strand when I was there. A judge had reached the end of a long civil action. He told counsel that he would deliver judgement after the coming weekend. He worked on it at home, and returned to the court on Monday. Unfortunately, he had left his written judgement at home. When he told counsel of this, the following reply, no doubt helpfully intended, came from one of them:

'Fax it up, my Lord?'

'Yes,' replied the judge, 'I fear it does, rather.'

Or a time I remember as a very young barrister when a Queen's Bench judge who was rather past his sell-by date came on assize to Leeds. The jury were being sworn in to try a case before him. Part of the jurors' oath is to hearken unto the evidence. To everyone's surprise, when the testament was handed to one particular juryman he said, 'I can't do it.' The clerk to the court enquired why not. 'I'm deaf,' came the reply. 'How can I do justice if I can't hear properly?' The judge leaned forward, cupping a hand to his ear, and said to the clerk, 'What did he say?'

It was the same judge, I believe, who was presiding at a trial when a witness was asked by counsel what his first reaction had been when he was present at some traumatic event. Came the reply, 'I said to myself, well, I'm buggered.' The Judge asked the clerk of assize to repeat what the witness had just said. A po-faced clerk said, 'My Lord, the witness observed that he was taken aback.'

———————

Enough of that sort of thing. The bench in a criminal trial is a very different life from the Bar, and often a very lonely one. The very nature of the job means that in court you are under constant scrutiny from many quarters – the victim and their family, the accused and their family, jurors, counsel and the media.

The judge should let the case run without intervention,

unless really necessary. It is counsel's job to conduct the trial. F.E. Smith KC (later Lord Birkenhead) was the most glittering advocate of his generation at the beginning of the last century. In one trial in which he was counsel, Smith grew exasperated with the interruptions by a judge of generally poor reputation, and made it plain. 'Mr Smith,' enquired His Lordship, 'why do you think I am here?' Came the instant legendary reply: 'My Lord, it is not for me to seek to plumb the unfathomable depths of divine providence.'

Once one becomes a judge, the camaraderie of chambers and Bar Mess is gone. Quite often, on circuit, a High Court Judge has no other judicial colleague with him or her to share the lodgings in the evenings. It can be a lonely time. There are some congenial occasions when a number of judges are together in a city, and (with luck) you get on well with them. (I can remember one lodgings where, remarkably, all three of us had been at Leeds Grammar School. At dinner, to the astonishment of the staff, we all rose as one and sang the school song – in Latin.)

One enjoyable dimension of appointment to the High Court that deserves separate mention is that it brings with it encounters with the High Sheriff of any county outside London where the judge sits.

The office of High Sheriff goes back to Saxon times, when the incumbent played an important role as the sovereign's representative in the county or shire, being responsible for the local maintenance of law and order, and for the collection of taxes. Today the office is essentially ceremonial. The High Sheriff is a royal appointment; he or she holds office for one year. Because the office involves a great deal of entertaining as one of the sovereign's representatives in the county, those who accept the job are invariably fairly well-off, as well as being best described as local notables. One of their principal duties is to see to the comfort and needs of any visiting High

Court Judge. They visit the judges' lodgings when any of the judges are resident, and they entertain them in their homes. They frequently sit on the bench with the judge during the disposal of cases. On court occasions (and on some others, as we shall shortly see) they wear ceremonial dress of black velvet coat and breeches, white lace ruffs at the neck and cuffs and (for men) a ceremonial sword in a large scabbard.

The duties discharged by the Shrievalty used to include the most demanding and melancholy one of attendance at the execution of a condemned prisoner. There is an anecdotal report of one such occasion a very long time ago, which is as good an illustration of black humour as I have ever encountered.

As the appointed hour approached, the condemned man was taken from his cell to be escorted to the execution shed. Protocol demanded that his companions in the procession should include the prison governor and the High Sheriff and his chaplain. The weather was terrible. As they crossed a large, cobbled courtyard under leaden skies, there was sleet in the air; it was bitterly cold. The prisoner, with truly astonishing stoicism, said to the High Sheriff, 'This is a grim day for a grim deed.'

'I don't know what you are complaining about, my good man,' the High Sheriff replied. '*We* have to walk back.'

On a (very necessary) lighter note, a very good friend of mine, the late Victor Watson, was High Sheriff of West Yorkshire. In that role, he visited a home for the elderly. Since he was to be involved in formally opening a new wing of the home, he wore his ceremonial robes. Afterwards, still berobed, he politely circulated among some of the residents. He bent down to speak to a very old lady confined to a wheelchair. 'Do you know who I am?' he asked.

'No,' replied the lady, 'I don't know – but if you ask Matron, I'm sure she'll be able to tell you.'

If, as a Queen's Bench judge, your sitting out of London coincided with the beginning of the new legal year (in the autumn), you attended a service at the local cathedral, accompanied by local dignitaries, and alongside the High Sheriff and his chaplain. And so it was that one October day I was bidden to do as much in the city of Leicester, and found myself in the back seat of a large Daimler. Between me and the partition separating us from the driver and my clerk in the front were two 'jump seats', very small folding seats that had to be folded snug with the partition after use in order to allow the back-seat passenger to get out of the car. On this occasion, the jump seats were occupied by the High Sheriff and chaplain, facing forwards.

We swept up to the cathedral entrance. There, six mounted policemen raised their bugles to announce our auspicious arrival. A police inspector sprang to attention, saluted, and opened the door to let us out of this impressive conveyance. Nothing happened. The High Sheriff, his back still to me, spoke with reddened neck and through clenched teeth: 'My Lord, I'm stuck. My scabbard's wedged in the seat mechanism.' The bugles had ceased their sound; there was an enquiring silence. The luckless man pulled and tugged until – oh, what relief – the scabbard freed itself, and the velvet-clad High Sheriff of Leicestershire was propelled violently sideways from the car rather like a human cannonball, into the arms of the inspector. The flustered chaplain followed, stumbling over his cassock as he stepped out. Then it was my turn to make the grand exit, in scarlet robes and full-bottomed wig. This scenario, now verging on pantomime, was overlooked by a scaffolding-clad building. As I emerged, I distinctly heard a bemused workman high upon the structure say to his mate, 'Well, it certainly ain't Father Christmas.' The law in all its majesty . . .?

It would be quite wrong of me to end this part of my

chronicle without saying how much I enjoyed my times with local Shrievalty and their spouses, how indebted my wife and I are to them, and how many happy memories of them we still hold.

———·+·———

I have already suggested that the lifestyle of a judge is markedly different from the independent and supremely individualistic life enjoyed at the Bar. The qualities demanded of a judge are quite obviously different from those needed at the Bar. It is also true that, for many, success in the latter does not make for a respected judge.

Overall, there is a distinction between life at the Bar and life on the bench that has a special resonance for me. A career leading to the bench is the very opposite in its implications of that applying to other professions, or in business. That is because in most areas, the higher you climb, the greater the freedom you enjoy. You become, more and more, your own man. In my profession, the very opposite is the case. The free spirit that invests life at the Bar with such attraction comes to an abrupt end upon judicial appointment. From then on, the pattern of one's life is dictated by others. Where and when you work, and the cases that you undertake, are not of your choosing. Your total independence in court is a 'given', but in a very real sense you have become an employee. My father would have deplored it. Overall, it will not surprise you to know that when I look back on my initial elation at my appointment I recall the aphorism warning us that to travel hopefully is frequently better than to arrive.

Finally on this subject, you have to remember that life as a Queen's Bench judge in my case dictated an almost ceaseless diet of major crime. Eventually such a diet can lead to intellectual indigestion. Whatever the public fascination with violent death, sexual perversion, or corruption in high places, long-serving judges rarely see it that way. Cynicism holds sway. A judge begins to see all life as a four-letter word. Boredom sets in, and a bored judge is a bad judge. I was no exception to those afflictions, and so when that time came I decided to quit. The long legal vacation in the summer before I sat for a final winter term gave me the chance to reflect on some of the things that have imbued in me my deep pride in, and devotion to the English legal system, and it is to these that I shall now turn.

7

AT THE END
OF THE DAY . . .

Despite the movement towards fusion of the two sides of
the legal profession – solicitors and barristers – it is my
conviction that a healthy, independent Bar is an essential
buttress to the rule of law that defines any nation as civilized
and well-ordered.

Trial by jury remains the best vehicle for determining guilt
in major criminal cases. A judge sitting alone or with assessors is bound by the letter of the law; a jury is not. A jury
can simply cast aside a legal principle and conclude, 'We
don't care what the law says; this is not fair.' On another
point, those who suggest that some issues in today's world
have become so complex that they would elude a jury's
understanding are aiming at the wrong target. It is within
the competence of counsel of quality to deal with that
complexity, and it is their duty so to frame the charges and
present them in a way that a jury can understand – and,
believe me, they will understand.

Moreover (as I said much earlier) a jury represents the
voice of society in matters of supreme importance to all of
us. It is a voice that is highly relevant to the criminal trial
process, and one, in my opinion, that demands to be heard.

The nature and burden of proof beyond a reasonable
doubt has long been the 'golden thread' that runs through
English criminal jurisprudence. That specific and graphic

metaphor, first enunciated in a case decided in the House of Lords one year before I was born, is a guiding light that has illuminated the way to justice for countless generations. It is the jewel in the crown that forms our criminal law.

Prison as punishment presents a permanent conundrum. In 2017, the Justice Secretary announced that two new prisons were to be built, observing elsewhere that this might help to cure the incidence of reoffending. The logic of this entirely eludes me. For a few, no doubt, being locked up is a deterrent experience that never leaves them. For many, it is a brutalizing experience and one that serves as an apprenticeship in crime. And, furthermore, there is this: it may come as a surprise to some people to learn that for a large number of prisoners 'time inside' is a welcome respite from the burdens of responsibility that freedom carries with it. No doubt, especially for these institutionalized beings, a more 'modern' environment will enhance the charms of a fresh sentence.

I remember an old lag with a string of convictions and prison sentences who, on the very day of his release from a substantial prison term, smashed the window of a jeweller's shop in Bradford and took several rings from the display. He made no effort to escape. At the city Quarter Sessions, he chose to represent himself and submitted to the Recorder of Bradford, Bernard Gillis QC, that with his record the public interest demanded the imposition of a long sentence for their protection. The Recorder knew what the prisoner was about. 'The best I can do for you, my good man, is a sentence of four years.'

In sum, the utility of imprisonment as a socially effective instrument is highly questionable. The only certainty is that it keeps the truly dangerous offender out of circulation. If we expect more, then I suggest that we are always likely to be disillusioned.

The opinions of experts should always be treated with caution. There are innumerable instances in our legal history where such opinions have caused miscarriages of justice, often when too late for effective remedy. A measured scepticism is the right approach to expert opinion, and judges should be astute to urge this upon juries.

Corruption is a vice that is ever present in society, and is classless. We who are fortunate to live in this sceptred isle are inclined to believe that our standards of public life offer a model of rectitude to less fortunate nations. My professional experience suggests that we should be very careful to avoid complacency on this score.

As regards 'stale' cases, I urge the strongest possible caution be exercised in decisions to prosecute in what these days are called historic cases.

In this context I need no reminding of the seriousness of paedophilic crimes. They are very grave, and their impact on their victims is often life-long. The authorities are under great pressure to be seen to be doing something. But in offering this warning as I do, it is necessary to bear in mind that there is more than one prospect of a miscarriage of justice here. First, such allegations mean that to meet them when they are so old, it may well prove impossible for an innocent suspect to offer an effective defence. He – and others who might otherwise have been his witnesses – may have no recall of highly relevant matters. Documents may be long gone. The second danger lies in the bandwagon effect of the notoriety of some of these allegations. I suggest that it is now abundantly clear that dishonest fantasists may and do seek a slice of the action by making false accusations. Others may simply be after compensation. The irrevocable mischief and distress caused to the lives of public figures by totally fabricated stories cannot be overstated. Some of those at whom the finger is pointed (or their loved ones) have died under a stigma that is withdrawn only later. What real comfort can there be in a posthumous apology?

I also want to say that it is my view that those who are suspected of sexual crime, in particular, should remain anonymous at least until charged. The identity of the complainant is normally protected in perpetuity. Surely in these cases the person accused is entitled at least to some degree of protection? It is a difficult line to draw.

And now, finally, to some thoughts that were lent greater force shortly before I completed this memoir, by way of the Referendum leading to this country's ultimate exit from the European Union. They are however rooted in the whole of my life's experience and so I make no excuse for laying bare my soul here. I am not expressing any view about the generality of our ties with Europe, but I believe that my decades in the law do entitle me to say something about our legal system and its national identity.

I sing 'Land of Hope and Glory' with fervour and with pride, but I am not blind to our frailties; I am not a xenophobe. That said, it is now some 800 years since Magna Carta was exacted from King John at Runnymede. Cynics would say that it was more a licence to the barons of England than a bill of rights for the common man. But it seems to me that it has been adopted through those many centuries for a much wider purpose. That is not surprising, since the Great Charter itself proclaims in timeless words: 'To no one will we sell, to no one delay or deny right or justice.'

Since the thirteenth century, the rule of law in this kingdom – principally through the unique medium of the common law – has adapted and changed in an infinite variety of ways. By this means our individual liberties have been protected and, where necessary, enhanced. This structure of liberty has protected our rights in a manner which excites envy, world-wide admiration, and imitation.

Trial by jury, the burden of proof, habeas corpus and the adversarial system are but a few examples. Looking at the European emphasis on human rights leads me to the following conclusion. No citizen within these shores has ever needed or sought to have his freedoms defined or constrained by any definition of human rights. Our rights are limitless, unless prohibited. They are presumed – not defined. The yeoman of England stands tall, arms akimbo, and says, 'Show me where it says I *can't*.'

Rudyard Kipling has it for me:

> And still when mob or monarch lays
> Too rude a hand on English ways
> The whisper wakes, the shudder plays
> Across the reeds at Runnymede
> And Thames that knows the mood of kings
> And crowds and priests and such like things
> Rolls deep and dreadful as he brings
> Their warning down from Runnymede.

By all accounts, Kipling had his failings, but with those words he uttered a siren call to be proud of our legal inheritance. Count me in.

EPILOGUE

On a summer day in 1999 I wrote to the Lord Chancellor, Derry Irvine, telling him of my wish to retire at the end of the year – the dawn of a new millennium. I had been exceptionally fortunate to spend my working life in my chosen profession. It had proved to be a life of challenge, fascination and fulfilment. I have always believed that in our journey through this world it is important to recognize when the time has come to turn the page, to move on. This was the time.

I chose to sit on circuit at Leeds for the last six weeks of Michaelmas Term 1999. On 19 December 1999, in a Leeds courtroom, two members of the local Bar bade me farewell on behalf of the Circuit. (By happy chance, one of them, James Goss, is himself now a High Court Judge.) Through them, I gave my thanks to the Circuit and all the Bar for what they had given to me over so many years. I spoke of my deep gratitude to my wife and my family for their loving support through some testing times. Then it was time to go. I stood up. My clerk recited for my last time, 'God save the Queen and my lords, the Queen's Justices.' I bowed to counsel, and left the room. I was 200 yards and forty years away from the staircase I had climbed as a new pupil in Vince's Chambers.

Before I bring these meanderings to an end, I wish to record what was for me a remarkable event that took place when I was nearing their conclusion. Oscar Wilde said that life imitates art. Why do I mention that? A distinguished QC and former leader of the North-Eastern Circuit, John

Elvidge, very recently received a letter from a lady named Lynda Horsfall, living in Australia. She had emigrated there in 1982, and had only recently learned of the death of Gilbert Gray, which is what prompted her letter.

It seems that some forty years ago, as a very young shorthand writer, she was working in a court in Leeds where GG was one of several counsel involved in a case of compelling boredom. She saw that he passed some time idly sketching. When the court rose at the end of the day, it seemed that he had discarded the sketch, so she asked if she could have it. The artist readily agreed. She was, and remains, so taken with it that she had it framed, and it still hangs in her home in Canberra.

Her letter to John Elvidge told that story, and expressed her sadness at learning of Gilbert Gray's death. Enclosed with the letter was a copy of the sketch. She asked that it be passed to friends or family. Knowing of my tribute to GG at York Minster, it came to me, and it is reproduced below.

GETTING ON.

GETTING ONNER.

GETTING ONEST.

When I saw it, I recognized at once that in that skilfully sketched triptych was encapsulated the essence of my personal chronicle. I felt strangely, but very strongly supported in my long-postponed decision to write this memoir. It was as if my cherished friend was saying to me, 'Well done, Oggers. As your Prologue promised, you told it as it was.' And it came to me (I kid you not) at the very time when I was writing the passage about photographs that immediately follows this paragraph.

———•——

In my home in Yorkshire there are four framed photographs. The first is a black and white one of me in barrister's wig and gown, taken in 1959. An unlined face looks forward with naïve anticipation. The second is a full-length one in my Silk regalia – which, I have to say, betrays an unattractive degree of smugness and even a hint of pomposity. The third was taken outside the Law Courts in London on the day I became a judge of the High Court. I am fully robed in scarlet and ermine, and accompanied by Sally, my very dear wife.

The final image is one of me in my judge's chambers on the day that I retired, and wearing for the last time my robes as a Judge of the Queen's Bench Division. Looking at my face in that photograph still presents to me an enigma. For sure, relief is there, but perhaps also a wistful nod to so many exciting days that beckoned incessantly, and are now irrevocably gone.

In 1973, when I was sworn in as a QC, my then seven-year-old daughter looked at me in my Silk gown, knee breeches, silver-buckled patent leather shoes and full-bottomed wig, and said, 'It's only Daddy in disguise.' Well, all disguise is now long forfeit, but has been laid aside with infinite affection. (For a short time, I used the red robe as part of my Father Christmas outfit. The grandchildren were not deceived.)

To Greta Garbo, who by all accounts knew a thing or two, is attributed the wise advice that 'this life ain't no dress rehearsal'. On the stage that in a very real sense was the setting for much of my life, I did my best to honour that philosophy.

———·•·———

And now these reflections must end. In September 1978, a few months before he died, my father added the following to his compendium of 'Thoughts while Thinking':

> Only a handful of mankind can rise above the humdrum, day-to-day routine of existence. We pursue a shadow that starts with vain hopes . . .

When I re-read those words, I look back on the cornucopia of riches that filled my working life to the very brim. I wish that my dear dad were able now to read this, my journey down memory lane. Would he perhaps give a wry smile of acknowledgement that, at least in my life of crime as I lived it, his pessimism was confounded? I hope so.

ACKNOWLEDGEMENTS

I wish to record my indebtedness to some of those who helped me in restoring to life these forensic fragments of memory.

To my family:

Our daughter-in-law, Jo, who first pointed me in the right direction, knows how very much I owe to her. To our daughter-in-law, Ness, go my thanks for spurring me on when I faltered. To the youngest generation, because I first undertook this journey down memory lane to answer the question of some of our grandchildren, 'What did Pops do?' Now they know.

To Charlie Redmayne and David Roth-Ey of my publishers, for their initial encouragement from on high that meant a very great deal to me. To my copy editor, Steve Gove, and my project editor, Iain Hunt – thank you both for the painstaking work in dotting the 'i's and crossing the 't's. To my editor, Tom Killingbeck, I offer my special thanks for his patience, understanding and expertise in bringing this to fruition.

Finally, to all those at the Bar who were my colleagues, my adversaries, and my boon companions as fellow members of the North-Eastern Circuit. In my time with them lies the genesis of these recollections. To have spent most of my professional life with them was a rare and cherished privilege, and a source of unbridled pleasure. Some are still with us; some, sadly, are no more. All of them have my deepest and abiding gratitude.